DAVE PELZ'S
GOLF WITHOUT FEAR

How to Play the 10 Most Feared Shots
in Golf with Confidence

DAVE PELZ

WITH EDDIE PELZ AND DAVE ALLEN

GOTHAM
BOOKS

GOTHAM BOOKS

Published by Penguin Group (USA) Inc.
375 Hudson Street, New York, New York 10014, U.S.A.

Penguin Group (Canada), 90 Eglinton Avenue East, Suite 700, Toronto, Ontario M4P 2Y3, Canada (a division of Pearson Penguin Canada Inc.); Penguin Books Ltd, 80 Strand, London WC2R 0RL, England; Penguin Ireland, 25 St Stephen's Green, Dublin 2, Ireland (a division of Penguin Books Ltd); Penguin Group (Australia), 250 Camberwell Road, Camberwell, Victoria 3124, Australia (a division of Pearson Australia Group Pty Ltd); Penguin Books India Pvt Ltd, 11 Community Centre, Panchsheel Park, New Delhi–110 017, India; Penguin Group (NZ), 67 Apollo Drive, Rosedale, North Shore 0632, New Zealand (a division of Pearson New Zealand Ltd); Penguin Books (South Africa) (Pty) Ltd, 24 Sturdee Avenue, Rosebank, Johannesburg 2196, South Africa

Penguin Books Ltd, Registered Offices: 80 Strand, London WC2R 0RL, England

Published by Gotham Books, a member of Penguin Group (USA) Inc.

First printing, November 2010
10 9 8 7 6 5 4 3 2 1

Copyright © 2010 by David T. Pelz
All rights reserved

Photo credits appear on page 378 and constitute an extension of the copyright page.

Gotham Books and the skyscraper logo are trademarks of Penguin Group (USA) Inc.

LIBRARY OF CONGRESS CATALOGING-IN-PUBLICATION DATA
Pelz, Dave.
    Dave Pelz's golf without fear : how to play the 10 most feared shots in golf with
confidence / Dave Pelz, with Eddie Pelz and Dave Allen.
        p. cm.
    ISBN 978-1-592-40571-8 (hardcover)
    1. Golf. I. Pelz, Eddie. II. Allen, Dave. III. Title.
    GV965.P3936 2010
    796.352'3—dc22   2010034116

Printed in the United States of America
Set in Sabon and Meta, with display in Foundry Gridnik
Designed by BTDNYC

3 4015 07039 3929

Contents

DEDICATION

To Lil . . . who never holed a three-foot putt;
to Ed . . . who couldn't keep his drives out of the
right rough, trees, or water to save his life; and to
Nick . . . who, with a scratch handicap, has played
every tournament of his life in mortal fear of having
to face a shot from sand, I dedicate *Golf Without Fear*.
Your attitudes, respect, and love for the game have
been a great influence on me. I thank and love you
for that! And may this book help others who are
experiencing frustrations similar to yours with
a particular part of their game.

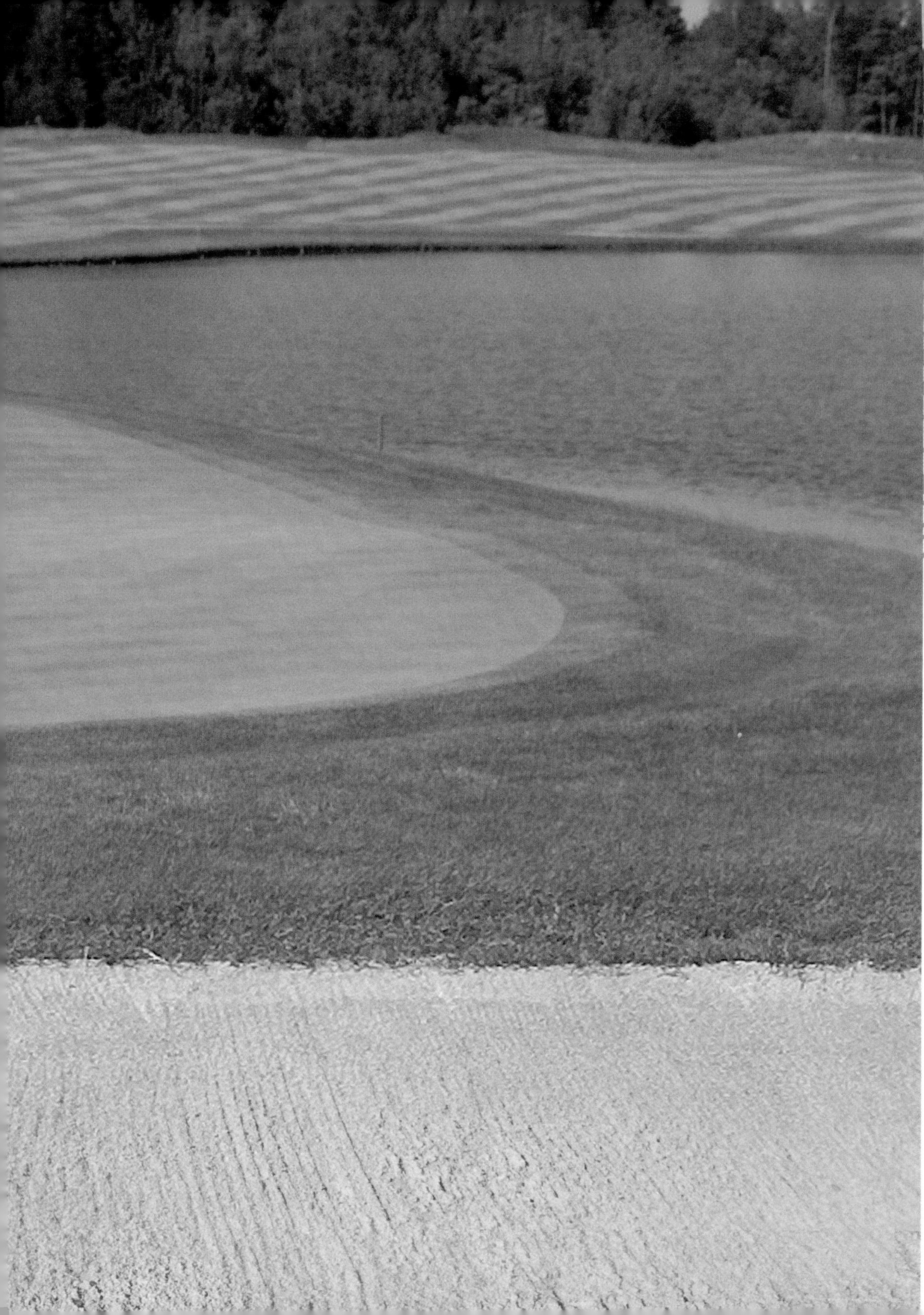

DAVE PELZ'S
GOLF WITHOUT FEAR

Purpose

THE GOAL

THE PURPOSE OF THIS BOOK IS TO ELIMINATE FEAR from your game. If you ever feel fear as you stand over certain shots on the course—anything from mild anxiety to cold, stark terror in your body—this is the book for you.

Millions of golfers have shots they fear. I see it in the eyes of golfers from rank beginners to low-handicappers to PGA TOUR professionals. As you probably already know, you can't play your best or enjoy your game to the max if you fear hitting shots as you address them.

In our schools, we can show you how to successfully play the shots you fear most. But first, let's see if this book can show you how to eliminate those fears in the comfort of your own home and backyard.

YOUR BENEFIT

Conquering your most feared shots will bring more enjoyment to your game; it will also help you lower your scores. As your confidence increases and your fears subside, your attitude and outlook will improve. Just as bad performances in one part of your game can snowball into other parts, the reverse is also true. As your worst shots become strengths of your game, you'll begin to play entire rounds without fear. And once you can play fearlessly, you can begin to play your best.

THE FIVE BASIC STEPS IN OUR PROGRAM ARE:

1. **Analyze** fear itself; open your mind to a change in the way you perceive a feared shot.
2. **Understand** the fundamental motions involved in hitting your feared shot, and what makes it so difficult.
3. **Learn** how to properly play the shot.
4. **Develop** your shot-performance skills in a nonthreatening environment (your home or backyard).
5. **Groove** (commit to habit) your new skills on the practice green or range at your course, then move to the golf course.

Understanding Fear

FIGHT OR FLIGHT

Understanding fear is the first step a golfer must take toward conquering it. Historically, fear is a condition humans experience when they perceive some sort of danger. The common reaction to fear is called the "fight-or-flight" response.

Mankind has been "fighting" or "fleeing" from fearful things since we hid in caves for survival. This fight-or-flight response is accompanied by the release of the stress hormone adrenaline into the bloodstream. A surge of adrenaline can make a weak man feel strong, as though he'd been injected with a powerful drug. Adrenaline is part of the body's natural defense against predators, invading armies, imminent threats (such as a three-foot putt to save par or extend a match) and many other "life or death" encounters. After experiencing a heightened level of adrenaline, some people describe the feeling as a good "rush" and will go to great lengths to create that rush again. Rush-seekers have been known to jump out of perfectly good airplanes, or to fling themselves off bridges with nothing more than a glorified rubber band to catch them, in search of that exhilarating adrenaline rush.

If your mind perceives fear, you will react to it. Fear of a shot in golf is often accompanied by sweating, an increased heart rate, rapid breathing, and shortness of breath. While golfers know that neither "fight" nor "flight" is an appropriate on-course response, their brains sometime command their bodies to tense or freeze up. Neither tension nor freezing up are good for the golf swing, but researchers say these responses are a natural reaction inherited from our ancestors (the freeze response was just as vital a part of early man's survival as fight or flight was). In other words, our fear reactions are in our genes.

Why does all of this happen? Experts say the reactions of stressed golfers are consistent with what we should expect from their ancestral gene pool, and as long as we have fear in golf we will have fearful reactions. They say there is no distinction between one's "natural" reaction to the anticipation of a disastrous golf shot and actual pain, embarrassment, or failure. From our perceived fears come the fear responses in our minds and bodies. Man has always reacted to fear, and apparently always will.

Why Do Golfers Fear Shots?

GOLFERS FEAR BOTH DIFFICULT AND EASY SHOTS

Many shots in golf—such as a ball buried deep in the sand—are difficult to play. Many golfers will experience fear when faced with such shots, usually because they require skills that the golfer may not understand or possess. Other feared shots, such as a three-foot putt, look simple enough, but create angst in golfers because they can be embarrassing when missed.

But the question of why some golfers perceive fear on the golf course while others don't remains unanswered. None of golf's difficulties (or failures) are life-threatening, so why fear a golf shot? The reality is, why you have fear doesn't matter. Whether your innate tendency to fear lies in your genes, depends upon the importance you attach to success, or is tied to your own self-image . . . it doesn't matter. If you fear a shot, you will have reactions to that fear, which will hurt your game! The important thing is to eliminate your fear (and fear reaction), play better golf, and increase your enjoyment of the game.

WHAT'S THE PROBLEM WITH PLAYING WITH FEAR?

Part of the problem of playing with fear is that no matter how the fear got there, it introduces both emotional and physical effects that undermine a golfer's chances of executing his or her swing to the best of their ability. In our "fear" surveys conducted over the last two years (more on this shortly), the overwhelming response shows that thousands of golfers are encountering shots they fear, and it's seriously damaging both their scores and their enjoyment of the game.

IS THERE A SOLUTION TO THE FEAR PROBLEM?

As golfers we can't eliminate our fear reactions when we fear a shot, because those reactions are in our genes. But we can eliminate our perception of fear for the shot and replace it with confidence. By eliminating the perception of fear, we automatically eliminate our fear reaction.

To overcome your fear, you must condition your psyche to stop perceiving a shot as dangerous. But how can you do that? Our way is to simply learn how to hit the shot successfully. This sounds simple, but as with many things in life, saying something and doing it can be two very different things.

WHAT'S THE TREATMENT?

To remove a preexisting fear, I believe you must change the normal perception you have of your ability to play. Normally you: 1) see the shot; 2) perceive fear because of the outcome you expect when you hit it; and 3) hit the shot (execute the swing) poorly. This process keeps making things worse. As a solution, I want you to leave the golf course entirely and go to an optimized place where you can work on learning to conquer the shot. This will facilitate your learning as you practice a new skill set, and remove any real scoring (or bad) consequences as you progress. By learning to hit shots in a safe environment—such as your backyard or den, where there are no scores to ruin—your learning can flourish.

Once you have learned the swing necessary to properly execute a shot that you previously feared, your mind and body will see and feel how your increased skills can better handle that shot. Then you can work on making that swing a habit (also known as "grooving" your swing) and conditioning your brain to play the shot for real—

first at home, then on a practice tee, and finally on the golf course. By following such a conditioning program, you can build confidence in your performance and overpower (replace) your old anticipation of failure.

It is important for you to understand that fear and confidence are at opposite ends of the "expectation" spectrum. So as your confidence increases, your anticipation of failure and fear will decrease. There is only room for one.

How to Use This Book

THE PROGRAM

Here in the introduction, I've developed a program to help you conquer your most feared shots. Then **I treat each of the "10 Most Feared Shots" individually (in reverse order of their fear ranking).** I've tried to make this book easy to read and use by keeping instructional text to a minimum and by using dozens of photographs to show how each shot should be played. In this regard, I hope what they say is true—that a picture is indeed worth a thousand words.

For each most feared shot, the "Fear Conquering System" includes:

1. The Shot (presentation, description, vision of the shot)
2. The Problem (shot detail analysis, what makes the shot difficult)
3. The Solution (how to set up, hit, and play the shot properly)
4. How It Should Look (how you should look playing the shot, including a "Golfer's-Eye View" perspective)
5. Success Examples (examples of how the pros get it done)
6. Conditioning Program (practice methodology, drills, feedback devices, and a road map to building confidence and removing fear)

THE SHOT

Every golf shot is unique, just as every golfer is different. Each of the most feared shots is defined with photos and an accompanying description to make sure you recognize and understand the shot. I have chosen photographs of shots that represent the fears detailed by our survey of golfers. If a particular shot that we've included is not exactly like the one you fear, examine it carefully to see if it would be close enough to elicit your fear if you had to face it. If it is representative, then proceed. If not, then go back to the list and pick another shot to work on.

THE PROBLEM

Each shot presents its own unique problems and difficulties. The fundamental details of what makes each shot difficult are described and explained. Some shots present distinct problems to particular golfers, while others expose generic deficiencies for many golfers. The point of this section is to help you understand the root cause of your problem with the shot you fear, because understanding is always the first step toward driving out and conquering fear.

THE SOLUTION

The solution section details the steps you need to learn to successfully play each shot. Here the fundamentals and skills you will later incorporate into your own swing mechanics are presented. In this section I try to create the mental image of the setup and swing changes you will need to make to execute the shot properly in the future.

HOW TO "SEE" THE "GOLFER'S-EYE VIEW™"

Once your mind "sees" how to execute a swing properly, it becomes easier for your brain to tell your body how to do it. But there is often more to "seeing" than meets the eye. In this section you will see and hopefully feel the way your body should set up to the shot, then internalize the swing you must make to hit it successfully. The better ingrained these images become in your "mind's eye," the better you will be able to re-create them with your muscles and body.

An important part of "seeing" shots in this section is our newly developed Golfer's-Eye View™, which shows you a view of the shot from a golfer's perspective. By this I mean that when you sit in your chair and move the book as described below, you will see the shot as you would if you first looked down at the ball and then up at the target—that is, as if you were addressing it on the golf course.

TO LEARN HOW TO SEE FROM THE GOLFER'S-EYE VIEW, CAREFULLY EXAMINE
THIS SHOT FROM DEEP GRASS, AND FOLLOW THESE FOUR STEPS:

1. Hold the book as you normally do, and examine the right-hand page closely; look at the stance, feet, club, and ball depicted in the photo. Imagine yourself addressing the shot.

2. Rotate the book 45 degrees clockwise, tilt your head to the left (for right-handers), and examine the left-hand page to see the target as you normally do when you look up from address and turn your head to look at the target.

3. Rotate the book back to horizontal and look down at your feet and ball again (on the right-hand page), just as you usually do during your pre-shot waggle.

4. Now look up again (rotate the left page up again) and take a second look at the target. Rotate the book each time you change where you look. Imagine your setup and how this shot would look and feel if you were standing over it on the golf course.

THE MAN BEHIND THE LENS (AND GOLFER'S-EYE VIEW)

On a more personal note, you may be interested to know more about how legendary golf photographer Leonard Kamsler developed the Golfer's-Eye View concept for this book (please turn to the Afterword, page 370, at the end of the book for more on Kamsler).

SUCCESS EXAMPLES

This section is provided to give you additional images to help your brain internalize the motions and positions required to play each shot properly. The more you view these images, the more likely they are to find their way into your mind's eye, and then out onto the golf course. Try to mentally internalize the swing motion as it will feel to you when you learn to make it. The more vividly you can "see" perfection in your mind's eye, the more successful your future swings will be.

CONDITIONING PROGRAM

After you have studied your feared shot from the comfort of your chair, and intellectually understand the problems it creates, the solutions, how it should look, and how you will learn to execute it properly, you will be ready to start the process of conditioning your mind and body to properly execute the shot. And once you've learned to hit it successfully, with just a little more repetition, you will be on your way to conquering your fear of the shot.

The 10 Most Feared Shots in Golf

HOW WE DETERMINED THE 10 MOST FEARED SHOTS

Although we have no way of knowing for sure which shots you (the reader) fear most, we have done our best to determine which shots are generally the most feared in golf. Over the last two years, the Pelz Golf Institute has conducted surveys of golfers from all different skill levels, asking the question: Which three shots do you fear the most?

We presented survey questionnaires to our website and blog visitors at www.pelzgolf.com, to the readers of *GOLF Magazine* and GOLF.com, and to our Twitter followers at twitter.com/dave_pelz. We also interviewed golfers in our Dave Pelz Scoring Game Schools and Clinics nationwide, contestants at the GOLF.com World Amateur Handicap Championship in Myrtle Beach, S.C., and professionals on the PGA TOUR. We were gratified to receive more than 10,000 responses to our questions from golfers worldwide, whose votes and descriptions determined the "10 Most Feared Shots in Golf."

The results of our research can be summarized as follows:

1. More than a hundred different feared shots were described in detail by the full handicap/skill range of golfers.
2. Thirty shots stood out as being mentioned more often than the others.
3. Ten of these shots were most frequently cited, and are dealt with in this book.
4. The number-one most feared shot is the easiest (technically) to play.

The severity of fear described by golfers participating in our surveys varied from "serious anxiety" to completely "frozen in terror." The fear ranking of the shots was determined by the number of fear-afflicted golfer mentions (votes/descriptions), not by player skill level. Many golfers described their fear of shots as being so acute that it developed into the "yips" (also described as a flinch or a jerk, or a complete inability to execute a swing or stroke). Short putts were the biggest culprit for developing yips in golfers, but many of the other feared shots also created yips in at least some golfers.

Start the Program

YOUR MISSION

Your mission, should you choose to accept it, is to conquer the shot you fear the most. This means replacing your fear of the shot with confidence in your ability to play it.

GET YOUR EQUIPMENT

Gather up the training aids and/or feedback devices detailed at the end of each feared-shot chapter (these devices are also described on our website at www.pelzgolf.com in the pro shop under products and learning aids) and take them to your backyard. Take this book, too, for easy reference, in case you forget the specific problem solution you need to work on.

Start working on the shot you fear most first, because that will help you improve and lower your scores fastest. If you're already good at something, lots of additional practice can only improve you a little bit; when you're bad at something, a little practice can generate lots of improvement.

SET UP IN YOUR BACKYARD OR DEN

Set up an area in your backyard where you can hit 20- and 30-yard shots without disturbing anyone. We recommend using a 4' by 4' SYNLawn synthetic grass "Fairway Mat" (www.synlawngolf.com), to save your lawn from divots (with a 4' by 4' by ¾" thick piece of plywood under it as your platform), shims to tilt the grass platform, and almostGOLF balls (www.almostgolf.com). These "backyard safe" practice balls remove the fear and danger of breaking windows, denting cars, or hurting people, which might happen if you used real golf balls. For putting indoors, you'll need several training aids and a carpet that's good enough for putts to roll on.

You'll also need a target (a stick, broom, laundry basket, etc.), various pieces of lumber, and several other artificial obstacles to simulate the hazards and other problem areas you'll have to deal with on various shots. More details on the backyard setup will be at the end of each feared-shot section.

PRACTICE AREA SAFETY TIPS

SWINGING GOLF CLUBS CAN BE DANGEROUS

Practicing golf is just as dangerous as playing golf. You can slip from a platform, carpet, block or chair, swing and hit yourself or others, and serious injury can occur. Equipment can be especially dangerous when wet. Please proceed with caution, at your own risk!

SET UP YOUR SAFE PRACTICE STATION

Remember—safety first! Make sure you've situated your learning station so no one can walk up behind you without your being aware of them. Be especially careful around small children and dogs. It's your responsibility to make sure no one ever gets hit or hurt by a swinging golf club or golf ball. Whether at the golf course or at home, please be careful when swinging a club.

You should also be careful to hit the almostGOLF balls away from people. Even though the balls probably won't hurt anyone seriously, I'm sure being hit and surprised by a ball would be irritating and should be avoided. These balls normally fly about $\frac{1}{3}$ the distance of a normal golf ball: that's not too far for wedge shots, but if you're practicing irons and woods, they can fly over 100 yards.

ALERT! PRACTICE AT YOUR OWN RISK!

The practice sessions in *Golf Without Fear* involve sloping surfaces, obstacles, unusual body positions, and intense club-resistant impacts. Many of the concepts introduced here will be new to you, so be sure to exercise caution. If you choose to perform any of the drills in *Golf Without Fear*, do so at your own risk!

Every golfer has their own unique physical problems, so consider your own specific limitations and proceed cautiously. Take it slow. Stretch and warm up before any practice session, and be careful not to injure your back.

At the end of the day, fear isn't always a bad thing, and you don't want to eliminate it from your life altogether. After all, fighting or running from an attacking lion or an armed assailant could save your life. And some level of anxiety is normal, and good, in golf. It can put you on alert and keep your shots out of harm's way. The purpose of this book is to eliminate your *FEAR* of a particular shot (or shots) and its associated reactions, which you associate with bad results, and higher scores.

Don't be discouraged if after practicing your most feared shot in your backyard, you still fear that shot when you get to the course. Conquering your fear may require that you repeat several cycles of successful performance at home and on the practice range before it transfers out onto the course for good. But I promise you, your practice time will be time well spent, and success on the course will come. And in the end, while fearing a shot has no redeeming value . . . the rush of *conquering a feared shot* will greatly improve your enjoyment of the game!

It is a proven fact that with the right conditioning, all fears can be eliminated. Believe it. It's been done. You can do it, too! Now let's get on with conquering the shot you fear the most!

The Shot

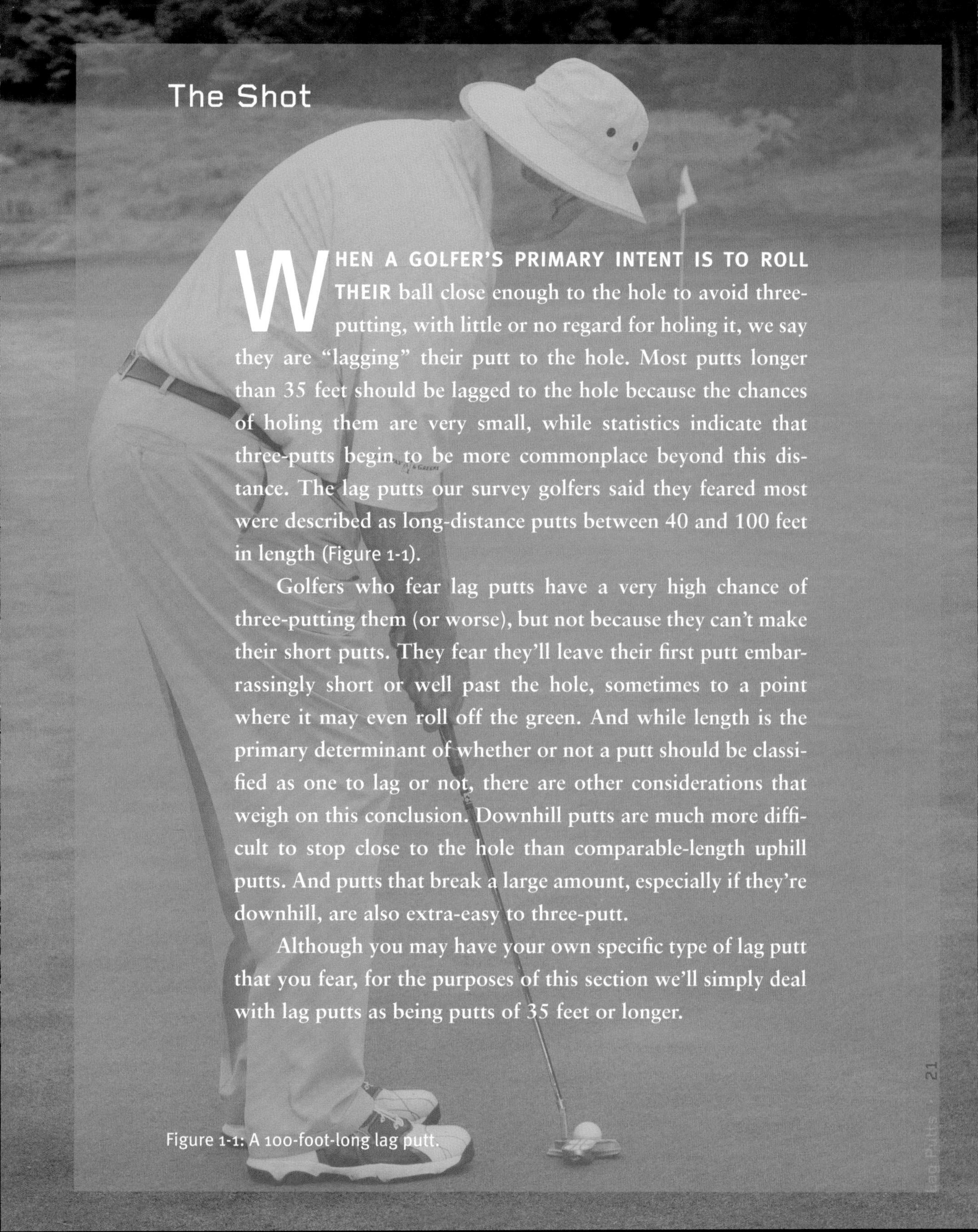

WHEN A GOLFER'S PRIMARY INTENT IS TO ROLL THEIR ball close enough to the hole to avoid three-putting, with little or no regard for holing it, we say they are "lagging" their putt to the hole. Most putts longer than 35 feet should be lagged to the hole because the chances of holing them are very small, while statistics indicate that three-putts begin to be more commonplace beyond this distance. The lag putts our survey golfers said they feared most were described as long-distance putts between 40 and 100 feet in length (Figure 1-1).

Golfers who fear lag putts have a very high chance of three-putting them (or worse), but not because they can't make their short putts. They fear they'll leave their first putt embarrassingly short or well past the hole, sometimes to a point where it may even roll off the green. And while length is the primary determinant of whether or not a putt should be classified as one to lag or not, there are other considerations that weigh on this conclusion. Downhill putts are much more difficult to stop close to the hole than comparable-length uphill putts. And putts that break a large amount, especially if they're downhill, are also extra-easy to three-putt.

Although you may have your own specific type of lag putt that you fear, for the purposes of this section we'll simply deal with lag putts as being putts of 35 feet or longer.

Figure 1-1: A 100-foot-long lag putt.

The Problem

The fear of lag putts comes from several sources. For one, golfers don't know how hard to "hit" their long putts, and when they do strike the ball, they often don't connect with it solidly. They don't have a "feel" for how long these putts are, nor do they have any idea how to improve their lag-putting performance.

Contrary to popular belief, poor lag putting is not usually related to a problem in one's stroke mechanics. The Pelz Golf Institute has tested this phenomenon on numerous occasions and found that golfers' lag-putting woes are essentially unrelated to the fundamentals of their strokes (such as their grip, rhythm, amount of forearm rotation or wrist hinge, etc.), or the length of putter they employ in their putting strokes. Research also shows that while the repeatability of their stroke affects the quality of lag putting, the fundamental shape of the stroke path does not.

When golfers three-putt from a long distance, they are usually guilty of leaving their first putt more than four feet from the hole. This is caused by one or more of the problem areas listed in Section 1-1.

Section 1-1: Four main reasons that golfers three-putt from long distance

1. Golfers "hit" putts to control distance, without a good "feel" for how hard to hit them, especially under pressure.
2. Ball impact is scattered over the putterface, and energy transferred to the ball does not accurately reflect energy (effort) created in the stroke.
3. Depth perception is poor, providing no real sense of how long the putt is.
4. Lag putting isn't practiced enough, and when it is, it's done poorly, without the feedback necessary for golfer improvement.

By nature, lag putts traverse many parts of a putting green—including differently sloped areas and level changes. This challenges both professional and amateur abilities to judge distance *and* read greens. Figure 1-2 shows that while pros occasionally three-putt, this is definitely one of the areas in which pros distance themselves from amateur golfer performance.

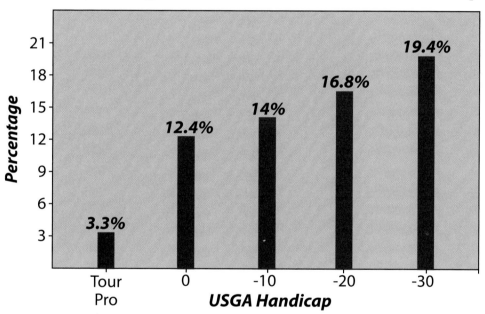

Percentage of Holes 3-Putted vs. Handicap

Figure 1-2: PGA TOUR ShotLink/Pelz Golf Institute Research: Amateurs three-putt about four to six times more often than TOUR Pros

The Solution

In lag putting, performance does not correlate with whether you putt with a short, conventional, long, or belly putter, or a conventional, claw, or left-hand-low grip. There are golfers who use all of the above and lag putt very well. If you don't consistently roll your first putt close to the hole, it's probably because of one or more of the four problems listed in Section 1-1 above. So don't blame your "God-given feel," your putter, or your putting style for your lag-putting woes; that is as ineffective as blaming the messenger when you don't like the message he brings.

The way to conquer your fear of lag putting is to improve the deficient skill areas in your putting that cause you problems. In the long run, these are the skills you must master for lag putts: You must be able to create strokes that accurately relate to the length of the putts you face, transfer a repeatable percentage of energy from your putter to the ball at impact, gauge the true length and speed requirements of putts with precision, and establish a regimen for practicing lag putts that will build green-reading confidence and consistency.

In short, you need the solutions listed in Section 1-2.

Section 1-2: A program for better lag putting

1. Create a pre-putt routine and ritual for building consistency in the rhythm of your lag-putt stroke.
2. Stand more upright to judge ("see") the length of your putt using binocular vision.
3. Use a "chip-putt" technique, which will be explained below.
4. Use the length of your putting stroke (instead of how hard you hit putts) to determine the distance your putts roll.
5. Establish a consistent ball-impact pattern centered on the sweet spot of your putterface.
6. Play lag-putt games to improve your "touch for distance" and green-reading.

Now let's look at these solutions one at a time and make sure you understand them. Then later, in our conditioning program, we'll detail how you can best achieve each solution and what kind of practice regimen you'll need to drive fear from your future lag putting.

This concept is simple: You shouldn't run up to your ball without looking at the green, then immediately stop and attempt to roll a dangerous, 60-foot down-and-sidehill putt to the hole. The physical exhaustion and maximum heart rate created by your dash to the ball, along with the lack of green-reading knowledge caused by a complete disregard for the slopes and contours surrounding your putt, will not prepare you to execute your best, most rhythmic, and most accurate putting stroke.

A better way to prepare for future lag putts is to execute a pre-planned approach. Your pre-putt routine should be designed to initially prepare you both physically and mentally to make your best possible stroke, with good rhythm and feel for the touch required, and then finally to learn from each putt you roll (for the benefit of your future putting). Such a routine, the essence of which is outlined in Section 1-3, starts as you read the green and imagine how your ball will track to the hole.

Section 1-3: A good putting routine

1. **See it** (walk around and evaluate the length, slope, contour, and probable speed of the putt).
2. **Feel it** (focus on the size and intensity of several practice strokes as you imagine the stroke required to roll the putt at perfect speed).
3. **Do it** (execute your putting ritual as you repeat your last practice stroke and strike the putt).
4. **Learn from it** (watch the ball roll and feel the correlation between your stroke action and its result).

Just before step No. 3, you should fall into your putting ritual (Section 1-4). This will help your mind and body execute your best possible stroke rhythm by taking advantage of the habit formed from numerous previous repetitions.

1. Your putting ritual should be executed in a rhythmic cadence.
2. The first three beats should be accompanied by small but always repeatable physical motions.
3. Beats four and five should consist of your putting stroke backswing and through-swing, respectively.
4. During beats six and seven, as you hold your finish and watch your putt roll, you should check your follow-through and correct it if necessary.

IMPROVE YOUR DISTANCE PERCEPTION BY STANDING MORE UPRIGHT

When humans stand straight up and look directly ahead with both eyes level and horizontal to each other, they use what is called "binocular" vision. This is the way we normally see things as our eyes focus on objects and calibrate their distance from us. Because it is the way we stand and look at things most frequently, and because experience allows us to get good at doing it, our perception of distance is optimized on golf greens when we use binocular vision. On the other hand, our ability to judge or "see" distance tends to be very poor when our head is down and our eyes are tilted vertically as they are in our traditional putting stance, because we seldom view objects that way.

The best way to gauge a putt's length is to stand tall and look at the hole with binocular vision—I've watched many great putters do this at one time or another during their pre-putt routine. As a result, I've incorporated it into my normal lag-putting posture (Figure 1-3). Instead of bending over long putts (left image) I now stand more erect and look at the hole between my practice strokes with almost-binocular vision. On particularly difficult putts I stand straight up and give the putt a completely binocular look. Then as I move into my final address position and get ready to putt, I try to retain as much of my upright posture (right image) as is comfortable. My last look at the putt is from an almost-binocular view, out along the putt line and to the hole.

Figure 1-3: It's easier to judge distance when your eyes are more horizontal (right) than when they are almost vertical (left).

Figure 1-4: My almost-binocular setup for lag putting prepares me to chip-putt.

From a face-on view (Figure 1-4), I use almost-binocular vision to "see" the length of lag putts. This helps me dial in the stroke length I need. And because you've practiced lots of long chip shots in your life and developed a good feel for them, you can probably lag putt with your chipping-swing motion better than you can with your putting stroke. I call this chipping with your putter, or chip-putting. In our schools we find that using your putter with a chipping swing from a chipping stance gives most golfers better feel and more accurate distance results on lag putts.

The concept of controlling distance by controlling the length of your putting stroke is so simple that most golfers overlook it. Instead, they tend to control the distances their putts roll by how hard they "hit" them. They hit short putts easy and long putts hard, using the muscles in their hands and wrists to control their effort. But gauging exactly how hard to "hit" a putt is a difficult thing to do, especially when you're excited or fearful, adrenaline is pumping through your body, and your hand muscles are stronger and tighter than usual.

A better way to control putting distance is to use the old "pitching pennies" approach. To understand this, look at how I pitch pennies to two lines on the putting green (Figure 1-5). One line is four feet in front of me; the other is 40 feet away. As I stand in the same spot using only my arm swing to pitch a penny to each line, can you tell which image shows me pitching a penny four feet? Of course you can: The short arm swing in the left image could only pitch a penny four feet, while the long arm swing in the right image has a good chance to toss it 40 feet.

Figure 1-5: The length of my arm swing controls the distance I pitch a penny.

In these two images, imagine the speed my hand is traveling when it releases each penny: on my short arm swing (left image), my hand obviously travels much slower than on my long arm swing (right image).

Now imagine that my arm is the shaft of your putter and my hand is the putterhead. In a short stroke, the putter travels slowly at the bottom of the swing arc. When you make a long stroke, however, your putter travels much faster through its arc bottom. That's the concept: Short strokes for short putts, long strokes for long putts.

This technique will give you a tremendous advantage in terms of distance control over "hitting" putts, because you can't see or feel a "hit" until it happens. When you control distance with the length of your stroke, however, you can see and feel your stroke length during your practice stroke (no matter how much fear or pressure you're under). By making several practice strokes you can dial in what looks and feels to be the perfect stroke length, before you actually use it. Then once you've seen the perfect practice stroke, you can repeat it for your real stroke.

REPEATABLE ENERGY TRANSFER REQUIRES REPEATABLE BALL CONTACT ON THE PUTTER SWEET SPOT

The amount of energy a putter transfers to a ball depends on 1) how fast the putter is moving and how heavy it is and 2) where on the putterface the ball makes contact. If a golfer makes three putting strokes at identical speeds, but contacts the ball in three different places along the face, the putterface will twist a different amount each time (Figure 1-6), and each ball will receive a different percentage of the swing's energy and roll a different distance. The farther away from the sweet spot (the exact point at which zero twist occurs: the center stroke in Figure 1-6) a putter makes contact with the ball, the more the putter will twist and the less energy will be transferred to the ball. Maximum energy is transferred to a ball if contact is made exactly on the putter's sweet spot.

By all measures, more consistent distance control can be achieved by grooving your putting stroke on your putter's sweet spot.

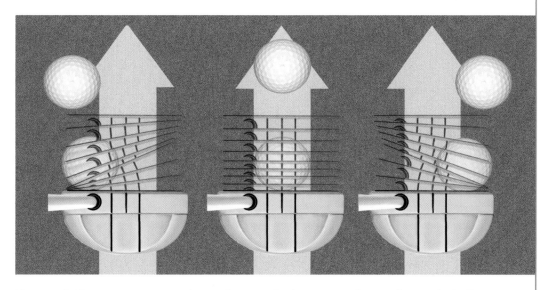

Figure 1-6: The more a putter twists at impact, the less energy it transfers to the ball.

This is confirmed by test records of putting-impact variations measured in our Dave Pelz Scoring Game Schools. When the putting-impact patterns of students are correlated with handicap (Figure 1-7), you can clearly see that better putters have smaller impact patterns, which are grooved more closely to their putter's sweet spot. What you need to learn from this is a fact of putting success: The more tightly your impact patterns are gathered around the sweet spot, the lower your handicap will be. And of course the opposite is true: The more scattered and random your impact pattern, and the farther from your putter's sweet spot it is centered, the higher your handicap will be.

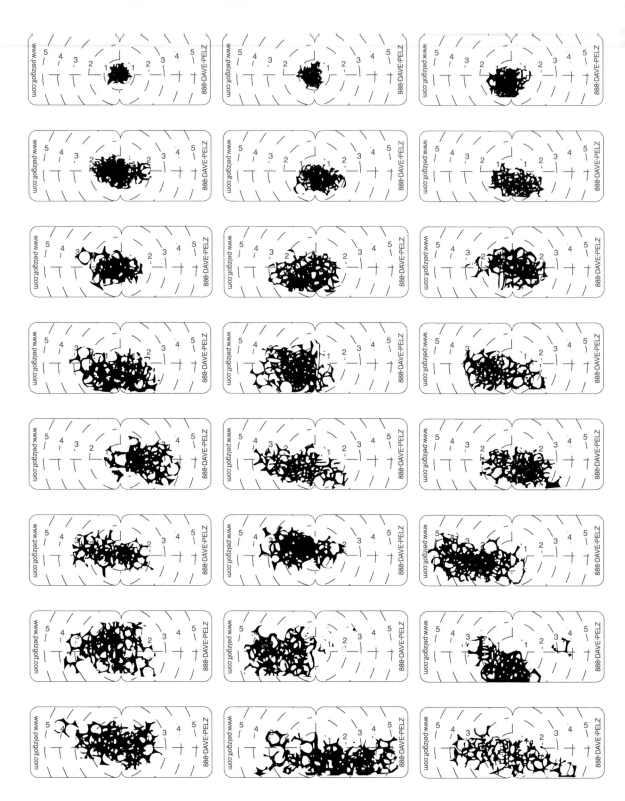

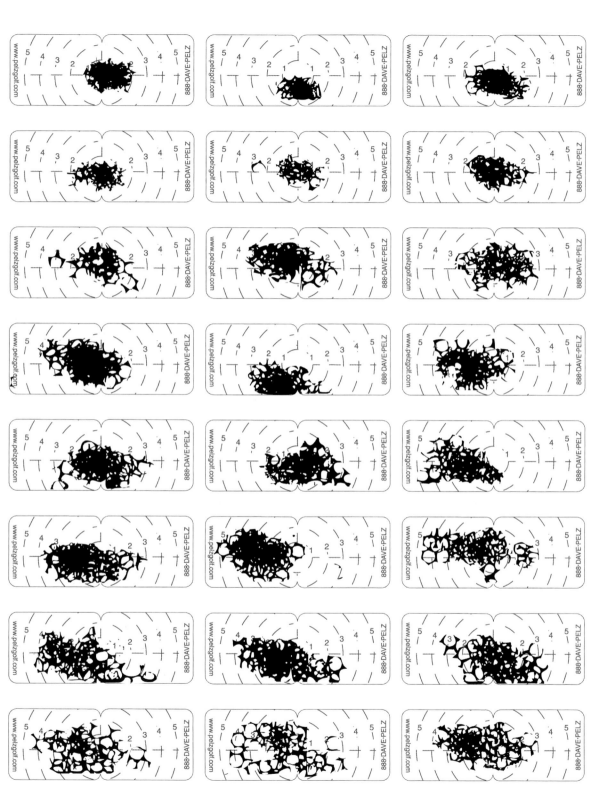

Handicaps range from lowest (top left) to highest (bottom right).

PLAY LAG-PUTT GAMES TO IMPROVE
"TOUCH FOR DISTANCE"

Practicing lag putting is essential to improvement. But most golfers don't spend enough time working on this area of their game, and even when they do, it doesn't seem to help much. The reason for their lack of improvement is that they practice without forming the habits and skills needed for good lag putting. They don't use a pre-putt routine or putting ritual, they don't work on improving their distance perception, and they don't use sweet-spot feedback to learn to groove their stroke contact for consistent energy transfer.

However, once you learn to use the length of your stroke to determine your putt distance (instead of just "hitting" the ball), sharpen your distance perception, and control your impact pattern consistency—along with playing the games we suggest later in our conditioning program—you will see measurable improvement in your lag putting . . . guaranteed.

How It Should Look

As you look at the ensuing pictures, remember that you are going to incorporate the three essential elements of good lag putting into your repertoire. You will 1) use the length of your stroke to control the distance your putt rolls; 2) strike the ball solidly on the putter's sweet spot; and 3) stand up straighter, like you do when chipping from the fringe, so your depth perception will improve through binocular vision.

In Figure 1-8, you'll see my normal putting posture and grip for putts inside 30 feet; please notice how I grip down on my putter several inches (inset). Now compare this to my more upright

OPPOSITE PAGE: Figure 1-8 and inset: Posture and grip for putts inside 30 feet.

lag-putt posture and full-length grip as shown in Figure 1-9. Although you might think there is only a small difference in my posture between Figures 1-8 and 1-9, I assure you that once you make this change yourself, you'll feel what a substantial difference it really makes in your depth perception and ability to evaluate putt distances.

OPPOSITE PAGE: Figure 1-9 and inset:
Posture and grip for lag putts of 35 feet or more.

From the Golfer's-Eye View, your lag-putt (chipping) stance will be narrower and slightly more open to the target line (Figure 1-10, right-hand page). The important difference this stance makes comes when you look out at the target with your eyes positioned horizontally for binocular vision (rotate book clockwise, see left/top page).

Figure 1-10: Golfer's-Eye View of a 100-foot-long lag putt.

Now take a look at my chip-putting motion from a face-on view (Figure 1-11). Notice how much body rotation there is to my chip-putting stroke—it's substantially more than there is in my normal makeable-putt stroke. This generates more power if I need it, but more important, it gives me the benefit of all the chipping practice I've done over the years, in terms of touch for distance. Remember: Chips from the fringe are frequently the same length as long lag putts, and they require similar-length swings to produce the proper distance.

Figure 1-11: My chip-putting swing action from a face-on view.

You're going to enjoy this new method of lag putting. It's comfortable and easy to use, and it allows you to judge and feel the proper stroke length needed to roll your putt the right distance, before you actually stroke your putt. Once you acquire this feel in your practice strokes, you'll be more confident when you repeat the stroke for real. All you have to do is stand up and perceive the correct distance with your binocular vision, dial in your practice-swing length, then repeat your practice swing in your real stroke. The goal is to see your future lag putts roll up to the pin like mine does in Figure 1-12.

Figure 1-12: Incoming 100-foot chip-putt.

An Additional Shot (for the Ages!)

As I mentioned earlier, the chip-putting technique can provide your stroke with lots of power if you need it. The following proves this point. During a video shoot for the Golf Channel at the 2004 PGA Championship at Whistling Straits, I was positioned on the front of the incredibly long and large 18th green. The hole seemed miles away on what was one of the largest greens I had ever seen. The point of my vignette was to show what could happen to a player in the upcoming championship if he drove it into the rough on this 500-yard par-4 hole and could only get his ball out to the front of the green on his second shot.

I told the television audience that most PGA TOUR pros would likely three-putt from this distance. Having almost never practiced putts of this length, their touch wouldn't be good and they'd probably leave their first attempt well short. I then proved my point by leaving my first putt 50 feet short of the hole with the swing shown in Figure 1-13 (honestly, I rolled the putt more than 150 feet, and I didn't leave it short on purpose).

Figure 1-13: This chip-putt swing left my first putt 50 feet short on the massive 18th green at Whistling Straits.

You must understand: 50-foot first putts are lag putts, and you must learn to deal with them. But leaving a 50-foot *second* putt is absurd! Somewhat embarrassed at that point, I dropped another ball and decided to use the full power of the chip-putting technique. The rest is history: My 206-foot lag putt rolled up, down, left, and right over the slopes on the green, and finally "lucked" its way into the hole (Figure 1-14). The Guinness World Record people say it was the longest putt ever made on television, and I'm quite sure it was the luckiest. (If you know of a putt holed from longer than 206 feet on TV, please let us know at comments@pelzgolf.com.)

Figure 1-14: At 206 feet (almost 70 yards), the longest putt ever holed on TV.

Success Examples

Phil Mickelson is a tremendous lag putter because he does a lot of things really well from long range. Chief among these skills is his ability to accurately perceive the length of a putt before he strokes it (Figure 1-15).

Figure 1-15: Phil Mickelson uses binocular vision to "see" the length of this putt.

Phil also practices and dials in his touch for distance by consistently practicing known-length putts (notice the white tees in the green marking off distances to the hole in Figures 1-15 and 1-16).

Figure 1-16: Phil Mickelson practicing his lag putting.

He is also known to take this practice very seriously. Phil plays the "lag-putt game" and challenges himself to roll ten putts in a row (from three different distances) to within three feet of the hole without missing. When he does miss that cherished three-foot circle around the cup (see his caddie, Jim "Bones" Mackay, measuring any putt that's close, Figure 1-17), he starts over again.

Figure 1-17: Bones in the process of measuring Phil's lag putt. Did it stop within three feet of the hole?

Figure 1-18: The pressure is on as Phil attempts his tenth and, hopefully, final lag putt.

I mention how focused Phil is in practice, because it's important. By setting a goal of ten good lag putts in a row, and being serious about achieving that goal, it puts a lot of pressure on the last few putts (for example, after achieving numbers seven and eight, there is serious pressure on putts nine and ten). Of course, practicing lag putting under pressure is good preparation for putting well on the course. And when you're tired and want to go home after a hard day's work, the pressure on the tenth and final lag putt (Figure 1-18) can be substantial.

Practicing with good feedback is one of the required solutions to overcoming your fear of lag putts. I want to emphasize how important it is. As good as PGA TOUR players are at lag putting, they still have to practice arduously for hours on end to maintain their touch for distance. The four opposite page photographs (Figure 1-19) show Mickelson practicing his lag putting before all four major championships. Even though he plays more than twenty tournaments every year and practices almost endlessly, you'll still find him fine-tuning his lag putting before every tournament he plays.

Figure 1-19: Phil Mickelson practicing his lag putting at the four "majors." (top left) The Open Championship, (top right) PGA Championship, (bottom left) U.S. Open, and (bottom right) Masters.

Conditioning Program

INITIAL REGIMEN AT HOME

TO CONQUER YOUR FEAR OF LAG PUTTS YOU WILL NEED TO:

1. Create and commit to using a putting *routine* and *ritual* in all your future putting (practice and on-course play).
2. Stand in a more upright posture and use binocular vision for distance evaluation.
3. Use your chipping swing with your putter to chip-putt future lag putts.
4. Use the length of your chip-putt stroke to determine the roll distance of the putt: short strokes for short putts, long strokes for long putts.
5. Groove a consistent impact pattern on your putter's sweet spot for better distance control.
6. Play lag-putt games to improve your touch for distance.

The first three steps are to be accomplished by experimentation and trial, until you feel comfortable in your new posture, stance, ball position, routine, and ritual. It is important that you finalize and commit to all three of these requirements before you spend time grooving your stroke mechanics and touch for distance. Now let's get started.

STEP #1: CREATE YOUR OWN PERSONAL PUTTING ROUTINE AND PUTTING RITUAL

YOUR ROUTINE

Establishing a putting routine and a putting ritual will not, on its own, improve your lag putting. But you need to establish and use them anyway. They are like the box you keep that's full of treasures. The box itself is not a valuable treasure, but it contains all the treasures and enables you to find and enjoy them. Your routine and ritual will allow the lag-putting skills you develop in the future to come together in a coordinated assembly of actions. They will tie your motions together into the rhythm that will become your new and improved lag-putting stroke.

Before you putt, you should always read the green by looking at it from both sides of your ball (first from behind the ball, then from behind the hole) to evaluate the speed of the green, the amount of uphill/downhill slope, and determine how much power and break to allow for your putt. Once you've read the green, you're ready to continue your pre-putt routine of "Seeing It, Feeling It, and Doing It" (Figure 1-20). By this I mean the following:

1. **"See It":** Stand behind your ball and look along the imaginary line you expect your putt to roll on. See the line. This includes visualizing the line you want the putt to start on, and its curvature (if it curves) into the hole. Make two or three preliminary practice strokes to approximate what you think you'll need in terms of speed and power to roll the ball to the hole on that line. Look from your ball to the hole and back a few times. See the entire putt.

2. **"Feel It":** Next walk to the side of your ball and position your body about four inches from your final address position. Make several practice strokes to get a feel for the length of stroke necessary to lag the ball to the hole. Tell yourself this is a preview of the stroke you want to make. Feel the length of the stroke you want to make.

3. **"Do It":** Now move into your address position, start your putting ritual, and execute the stroke.

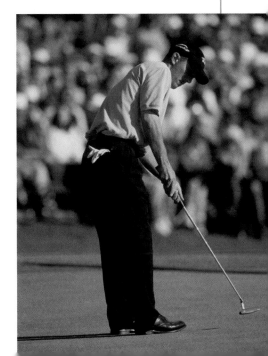

Figure 1-20: Mike Weir executes his stroke and holds his finish in his putting routine.

Every TOUR pro has a unique putting routine. The routine described above is my own, and it's okay if yours is different. But you must develop one before you spend significant hours grooving your stroke. A good way to start developing your routine is to pick a TOUR pro who has a personality and temperament similar to your own, then watch what he or she does before and after every putt. Try to use their routine as your own—but feel free to make a few personal changes for maximum comfort.

YOUR RITUAL

The last few physical motions you make before putting should be made in a "ritualistic" fashion, in the same rhythm and cadence that will set up and characterize the timing of your actual putting-stroke motion. You can establish this rhythm during your practice strokes by thinking (or saying under your breath) "one" as you swing your putter back, and "two" as you swing it through. If you do this for several practice swings, as you move your putter back and through (counting "one . . . two" each time), you will begin to see and feel the proper rhythm for your upcoming stroke.

As an example, I always prepare to start my putting ritual after I address my putt, with my putterhead slightly up in the air. As I touch my putter down on the ground behind the ball (Figure 1-21), I start to a count of "one" and say to myself "down." I then look up along my putting Aimline and think "look along the line" on the count of two. On the count of three I glance back down, press my hands a half-inch forward, and think "look down" at the ball. As I swing my putter back, making my backstroke, I think "back" on the count of four. Then I strike "through" my putt on the count of five. So my putting ritual starts and proceeds through impact to a count of five, as I think to myself: "down-look-look-back-through."

But I'm not done yet: I hold my finish (on the count of six) and check that my putterface is square to the Aimline and correct it on the count of seven if it's not. I then hold that finish and watch the putt roll. And that's my complete putting ritual: down, look, look, back, through, check, correct, to a count of seven, in the rhythm and cadence of my practice stroke. My actual putting stroke motion (backswing and follow-through) are simply parts four and five of the rhythmic ritual I execute now over every putt, out of habit. I don't even have to think about it, whether I'm putting on the practice green, in my den at home, or on the golf course.

Figure 1-21: My ritual starts as I touch my putter down to the ground.

You don't need to spend much time here, just enough to convince yourself you're comfortable standing behind putts, looking down the line to the hole while standing upright, and looking at them as you normally look at most other things. You need to learn that you are comfortable standing upright and using binocular vision to gauge putt distances. I'm sure this will feel natural to you from the beginning, since that's how you normally see the world.

THE WINDOW DRILL

If you're not as lucky as I am and you don't have a putting green in your backyard, you can still quickly evaluate how your binocular vision works compared to your normal "vertical eyes" vision from a bent-over putting stance. To do so, place several soda cans outside in your yard (or driveway) at different distances, so they're clearly visible through a window from a puttable surface (carpet) inside your home. Then set up near the window as if you were going to putt toward the cans (Figure 1-22). You only need one ball and a pillow to protect the wall.

I want you to putt twice to each can (into the pillow) using two different postures and strokes. Before each putt take a practice swing while looking out at a particular can, then address your ball and repeat that stroke exactly. First, from your old bent-over putting stroke, look at the can with your eyes in a vertical plane, make your practice swing and then putt. Second, stand in a more upright posture and make your practice stroke while looking out with your eyes horizontal, using binocular vision. Then again putt into the pillow. After going back and forth for a few putts of different distances, you'll see how much more comfortable it is to stand tall and use binocular vision to see and putt to distant objects.

Figure 1-22: The Window Drill allows you to putt in the comfort of your own home (looking at distant cans placed outside your window) into a pillow.

STEP #3: LEARN TO CHIP WITH YOUR PUTTER

THE CHIP-PUTT STROKE

From our Solutions section above, you know how and why to stand tall and chip-putt your lag putts. Now you need to discover how these two changes feel and how well they will work for you on the greens. The easiest way to accomplish this is to go to the edge of your backyard putting green or to a practice green at your golf course with your 7-iron and putter. Alternate hitting shots with your 7-iron from just *off* the green and your putter from just *on* the green, using the same stance and chipping-swing motions for both, to the same hole (Figure 1-23). Choose a shot of at least 35 to 40 feet or longer.

Figure 1-23: Hit your lag putts like you chip from the fringe, except use your putter.

STEP #4: COMMIT TO USING THE LENGTH OF YOUR STROKE FOR DISTANCE CONTROL

Here I'm asking you to commit intellectually to following the principle of "short strokes for short putts, long strokes for long putts."

It's as simple as that. As you look up at the hole during your practice stroke (always make at least one practice swing while looking at the hole), try to feel whether the length of your stroke is right for the putt, or not. Let your mind's eye judge whether it likes the stroke it sees and feels, relative to the putt you face. It's amazing how well your subconscious mind can perform this task, if you'll just let it do its job.

STEP #5: GROOVE YOUR STROKE ON YOUR PUTTER'S SWEET SPOT

MARK YOUR SWEET SPOT ACCURATELY

You are getting close to beginning to groove your new putting stroke, but you need to do one more thing before you start. You need to measure and mark your putter's sweet spot, so that all of your ensuing practice will be useful in training you to strike future putts solidly. Remember, the goal is to groove good stroke characteristics into putting habits.

To measure and mark your putter's sweet spot correctly, simply hold your putter up in front of you with the sole (bottom of the putterhead) parallel to the ground. Tap along the putterface with a sharp instrument (key, tee, etc.) until you find the point that makes the face move—but not rotate (Figure 1-24). The sweet spot is the place along the putterface that doesn't make the putter turn or wobble when you tap it.

Tap-tap-tap along the face about $4/10$-inch above the sole of the putter. Hold the putter lightly in your fingers so it can turn

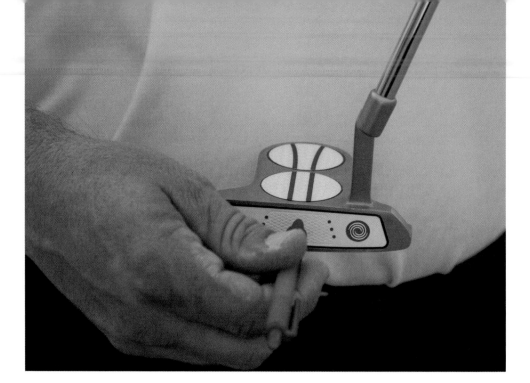

Figure 1-24: Tap-tap-tap along the putterface to find the sweet spot.

easily when you hit it out toward the toe or heel. This will make it easier to recognize the sweet spot when you do hit it and the putter doesn't turn. If your putter is not marked accurately, re-mark the putter's top line above the sweet spot with a marker or a file so it will be permanently visible as you address putts.

START GROOVING YOUR STROKE: THE INITIAL LAG-PUTT SESSION

As you start your stroke-grooving program, there is a feedback product you need to install on your putterface called Teacher sweet-spot tape. Shown in Figure 1-25, the strip of pressure-sensitive tape records where each putt is hit, and should be carefully centered on your putter's sweet spot before you hit any putts. With your Teacher tape in place, you are ready to begin grooving your lag stroke.

Enjoy your first few sessions indoors, putting balls into a pillow with long lag strokes (imagine that your putt is going to roll at least 40 feet without the pillow). Don't worry about where the balls go, just establish the good practice habits of standing tall, taking a practice swing before every putt, moving into your address position, and executing your chip-putt stroke within your putting ritual rhythm. Putt ten balls three times each (thirty putts) into your pillow, then take the Teacher tape off your putter. Mark and save each piece of tape with a date of practice; this will allow you to measure your progress—a reduction in the size of your impact pattern—over time.

Do this thirty–lag putt session four nights a week for two weeks. Each session should take only ten minutes. Use a new piece of tape for every session. After a few sessions you should begin to see improvements in your impact pattern. When the diameter of your impact pattern gets smaller than the #2 ring on the sweet spot tape, you're ready to move on to the next groove drill. As long as your pattern is still larger than the #2 ring, repeat the same drills four times for another week.

 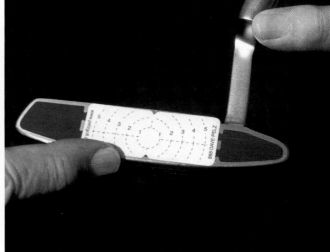

Figure 1-25: Use Teacher sweet-spot tape to record your lag-putt impact patterns.

CONTINUE LAG-STROKE PRACTICE WITH TEACHER CLIPS

Figure 1-26: Teacher® clips create three different tolerances around the putterface's sweet spot.

The next learning aid you need to install on your putter is called the Teacher putting clip (Figure 1-26). It can be installed and removed very quickly (it sticks on the putterface with double-sided tape) and has two prongs that will deflect the putt severely off-line if the ball is struck away from the sweet spot (Figure 1-27). While the feedback from Teacher clips is negative in nature, don't be discouraged. If you do these drills, I promise you'll start hitting your putts more solidly and your lag putting will improve.

Figure 1-27: Miss the putter's sweet spot and the clips will deflect the ball off-line.

There are three Teacher clips tolerances (Standard, Pro, and Super Pro), which can be used according to your putting skill level. Start your practice with the standard Teacher clip and make sure it's precisely centered on your putter's sweet spot. (This clip location is critical: It *must* be exactly centered on the sweet spot.)

Your indoor sweet-spot drill is to putt as many sessions as it takes with the standard tolerance Teacher clip (as detailed above, looking out the window at targets, putting into a pillow), until at least 50 percent of your strokes contact the ball solidly without hitting the Teacher prongs. Note: After further practice, when you get good enough to hit 80 percent of your putts solidly, move to the next tighter (Pro or Super Pro) Teacher clip tolerance.

STEP #6: PLAY LAG-PUTT GAMES TO IMPROVE YOUR TOUCH FOR DISTANCE

Once you get to a practice putting green, be it a SYNLawn backyard green like mine or the green at your local golf course, the real fun begins! To start your practice you only need to know about the lag-putt "safe zone" and the rules of the game. The safe zone for amateurs is the imaginary circle around the hole equal to the length of your driver (roughly a 43-inch radius). Any ball that stops within a driver's-length distance of the cup or touches the safe zone is considered "in" the safe zone (Figure 1-28). For pros, the safe zone is much smaller—equal to

Figure 1-28: The lag-putt game: The safe zone for pros is three feet in diameter, 43 inches for amateurs.

the diameter of a 7-iron with its head in the hole (a 36 inch radius). Whether a ball is in or out of the safe zone can be measured easily by laying your driver or 7-iron on the green with the clubhead in the hole; if the end of the grip touches the ball, the ball is considered "in" the safe zone.

To play the lag-putt game, walk off 40-, 50- and 60-foot reference distances from a hole, then mark each distance with a tee in the green. (In the case of the 66-foot putting strip in my backyard, these distances are marked by big rocks along the side.) The rules are simple: First, you must lag-putt three balls in a row into the safe zone from each distance without missing (Figure 1-29). When any putt does not finish in the safe zone, you must start over.

Figure 1-29: Here I am lag-putting on my backyard SYNLawn green from 50 feet.

Figure 1-30:
Thankfully, my
tenth lag putt
comes to rest in
the safe zone.

Then, to end the game, you must make a tenth putt stop in the safe zone from 50 feet (Figure 1-30). The tenth ball really puts pressure on your lag stroke, especially when you've been playing this game for an hour and you want to finish!

As you get better and better at the lag-putt game, your confidence on the course will grow and your fear of long putts will diminish. In time, if you keep this up, you *will* become a great lag putter! But it won't come easy. You must understand that it will take time, probably an entire golf season, to progress through the entire conditioning program detailed above.

But it will be worth the effort. When you stand on the 18th green needing a two-putt from 60 feet to win your club championship flight, and you roll your lag putt up to within a foot of the hole (Figure 1-31), you can proudly say YESSSSSSSSSSSSSSSSSS!!!!!!

Figure 1-31: YESSSSSSSSSSSSSSSSS!!!!!!

CHAPTER 2

Most Feared Shot #9: Against the Wall

The Shot

THROUGHOUT OUR FEARED-SHOT SURVEY, **GOLFERS** described their distaste for a shot they faced after their ball had rolled up close against some kind of object. Most often they described their ball nestling up against a fence, a tree, or a rock, which presented them with no option for a reasonable backswing or no room to swing the club through impact toward the hole.

During the writing of this book, I encountered the perfect opportunity to photograph just such a shot at the beautiful Hamilton Farm Golf Club in Gladstone, New Jersey. My ball had rolled up against the wall of one of their stables behind the sixth green (Figure 2-1), and as I contemplated playing the shot, I realized: This is it. This is one of the most feared shots in golf! It turned out to be the ninth most feared shot in our survey.

Figure 2-1: My ball bounced over the sixth green at Hamilton Farm Golf Club and snuggled up against the stable wall.

This ball position was exactly as so many of our survey participants had described. It allowed absolutely no room for a normal back- or down-swing (Figure 2-2) toward the hole. The obvious options for playing the shot were to hit it right-handed away from the hole (along the barn wall) into higher grass toward the out-of-bounds stakes, take an unplayable lie penalty (and drop within two club lengths and no closer to the hole in the long grass, which was no bargain), or walk back down the fairway and try the shot all over again (essentially losing two strokes). Out of respect for the wonderful Hamilton Farm Club and its members, we named this shot "Against the (Stable) Wall."

Figure 2-2: With my ball three inches from the wall, I had no room to make a normal backswing.

The Problem

Many golfers described their fear of this shot in terms of their anticipation of hitting themselves with the ball if they tried to hit it (most often chopping straight down on it). They described the penalty, the pain, and also their fear of hitting the ball twice. Several mentioned the possibility of hitting the ball on the clubface, then the hosel of the club, and then their leg.

There is in fact little chance that a right-handed golfer could swing right-handed at this ball: it would have to be a straight-down chopping action, unless you hit it straight along the wall in the opposite direction, away from the green. Limiting your swing in this situation to the normal "right-handed, toward the hole" parameters, however, is the cause of the problem. Sometimes under circumstances like these, you must think "outside the box."

A shot like this presents a problem that has nothing to do with poor swing habits or a lack of practice time. Instead, it has to do with a "ball-flight rule" that governs the relationship between golf swings and ball flight. Most golfers believe that a ball launches in the same direction that the clubhead swings through impact, and then curves as a result of the clubface being open or closed relative to that swing path. The old *PGA Teaching Manual* used to teach this, and many golf professionals have taught this swing path/ball flight relationship as gospel for many years.

This launch rule sounds reasonable, and seems to make sense. The ball will start along the clubhead path, and curve from there. So wherever your swing path aims, the ball will follow. Yes, it sounds reasonable, and it seems to make sense. But the problem is, the rule is wrong. The rules of physics are more important than the PGA's rules of ball flight, and physics say golf balls don't launch in the direction of a golfer's swing path.

The Solution

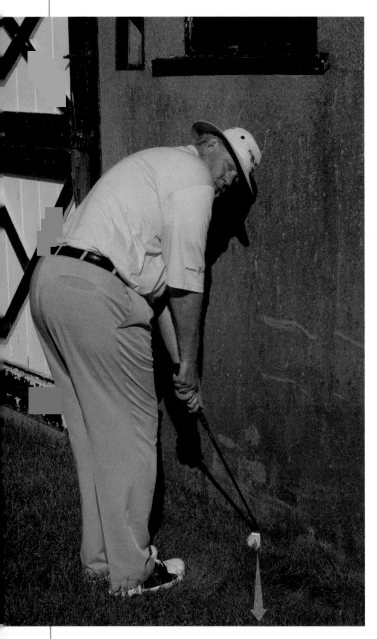

Figure 2-3: My left-handed swing along the wall (toe pointing straight down) aims the clubface and shot at the target.

In reality, golf balls launch in a direction almost perpendicular to your clubface at impact, *not* in the direction of your clubhead's swing path through impact.

This means that no matter what direction you swing the club through impact, if you can create a swing that contacts the ball *while the clubface is pointing toward the hole (or your target)*, your ball will fly essentially toward the hole. This is physics and reality: the ball will fly in whatever direction your clubface is pointing at impact, not in the direction of your swing path.

Clearly the only swing possible from this lie (with the ball positioned three inches from the wall) is on a path that parallels the wall. If I swing right-handed at the ball I can only hit it away from the hole, but then I might end up in a lie that's just as bad, or I might hit it out of bounds.

But look what happens if I turn around and swing left-handed along the wall (Figure 2-3). The proper solution in this case is to swing at the ball with a left-handed motion, turning my pitching wedge upside down (toe straight down) while aiming my clubface at the target. *Voila!* Because my clubface is pointing at the target, I can hit the ball there.

When you understand the reality of how a golf ball flies off of a clubface, you can hit shots in many new and exciting directions. The solution to hitting shots from against a wall (or fence, rock, or tree) is to understand the reality of ball flight, and then use it to your advantage.

How It Should Look

Holding this exact left-handed address position, if I turn away from the wall and face the camera you can see that my hands are close to being in a normal address position for a normal left-handed pitch shot (just a little forward of the perfect position, Figure 2-4). Facing the wall to make this left-handed swing looks and feels awkward at first, but I simply have to convince myself to make the best left-handed pitch swing I can muster and hope that I aimed the clubface correctly to pitch the ball toward the flagstick.

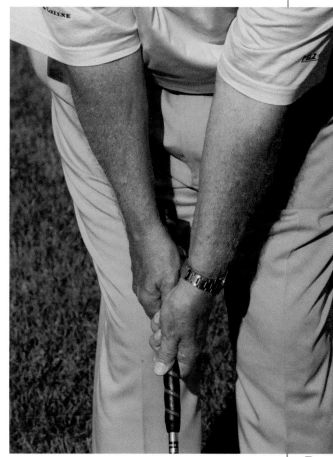

Figure 2-4: This shot from against the wall requires only a normal left-handed pitch swing.

Viewed from behind in Figure 2-5, there is nothing unusual about my address position or posture, except that the club is upside down. Otherwise, it looks as if I'm getting ready to hit a left-handed pitch shot.

Figure 2-5: If I had a left-handed wedge, this would be a simple pitch shot with the face closed.

Figure 2-6: My left-handed swing encounters no interference from the stable wall.

From a straight-down-the-line view, you can see that there's plenty of room to swing the club (Figure 2-6). The clubhead will travel parallel to the wall and encounter no interference from it, and the ball will launch off to the right. If the ball is hit solidly, it should fly toward the hole.

Looking down at the ball and the clubhead from the Golfer's-Eye View (Figure 2-7), this setup might appear strange to you. What really looks unfamiliar is the angle of the clubface, which points off to the right of the line you're going to swing along (i.e., your swing-path line).

But you can't let the strange look dissuade you from using the best shot to get the job done. Simply looking at a ball from a left-hander's address position used to seem really odd to me, but I've done it enough times now that it's no big deal.

Figure 2-7: A Golfer's-Eye View of a ball that's come to rest against a wall. Note the upside-down, left-handed pitching wedge setup, which will allow me to start the ball at my target.

Notice how easy this swing looks when you see it in action (Figure 2-8). If I were really left-handed and had a left-handed wedge, the shot would be so simple: I would toe-in (close) the clubface slightly and hit a nice little pitch shot. No problem. The truth is, despite the fact that I'm right-handed, I can make this left-handed pitch swing without much of a problem. I'm sure you can, too, with just a little bit of practice.

Figure 2-8: From a left-handed pitch swing along the wall, the ball launches perpendicularly off my clubface at impact and to the right of my swing line.

The reason most golfers don't attempt a shot like this is because they don't even know it exists. If you've never seen someone play this shot, or you don't sit around thinking about golf the way I do, you'd have no reason to think of or try it. But believe me, when you look up and see your little pitch shot, from this seemingly impossible predicament, roll up close to the flag for a potential par-saving putt with no penalty stroke involved (Figure 2-9), you'll be pleased you learned this shot.

The lesson to be learned from the shot against the wall is this: A ball essentially launches in the direction your clubface is aimed at the moment of impact. Knowing this will allow you to confidently play shots that you might otherwise be afraid to try with a conventional swing.

Figure 2-9: The left-handed pitch swing saves the day.

Success Examples

Imagine that your second shot came to rest next to this rock (Figure 2-10). Would you chip it forward to the right of the green and then hope to get it up and down for a bogey? No . . . not now! Not now that you know you can hit a shot that will launch in a direction perpendicular to your clubface at impact.

Enlightened by your new knowledge of the real "Launch Direction Rule," you can simply walk

Figure 2-10: The old rock strikes again.

behind this ball and visualize the line you want to start your ball on (Figure 2-11). Be sure to pick a spot along the line that's close to you (within ten feet usually works well), so that you'll have an easy time aligning the clubface when you get into your address position.

Figure 2-11: Find a spot (a leaf, twig, anything) along the line you want to start your shot on.

Address the ball with the clubface aimed directly at your desired starting line (Figure 2-12). In this case, you can see I've dropped my left foot back to make sure the ball doesn't fly into my left foot or ankle. While I've never actually hit myself with a shot straight off the clubface, it's better to be safe than sorry. I've found that I feel more comfortable over the ball—and hit better shots—if I drop my left foot back in this situation.

This ball was only two inches from the rock (Figure 2-13), and yet I could chip it toward the green by simply closing the face and swinging normally. You may worry about hitting the hosel on this shot, but the ball usually catches the clubface first. Still, I recommend you practice it a few times before trying it under the gun.

B e aware of the amount of loft on the clubface. You deloft the face when you close it down (aim left) and you increase its loft when you rotate it open (to the right). In this case, with the face aimed left and closed down, I had to use a very high-lofted club, a 60-degree lob wedge, to launch my ball on the trajectory of a normal 8-iron shot.

Figure 2-12: My setup doesn't look all that different from a normal pitch setup, except the clubface is closed and my lead foot is back.

Figure 2-13: A standard pitch-shot setup, except that the face is closed and delofted, and my lead foot is back.

Notice how the ball launches straight left off the clubface
(Figure 2-14), even though my swing path is parallel to the rock.

Figure 2-14: The ball starts left because the clubface points left at impact.

The result is another saved stroke, and not because I made a great swing or somehow pulled off a once-in-a-lifetime shot. I saved this stroke with an average swing because I knew the ball would launch in a direction perpendicular to the clubface at impact (Figure 2-15)—otherwise known as the Launch Direction Rule.

Figure 2-15: Knowing the Launch Direction Rule turns a scary situation into a simple pitch shot.

Conditioning Process

START WITH LEFT-HANDED SWINGS

You already own the key information you need—that balls launch perpendicular to the clubface—to conquer the "Against the Wall" shot. It's now time to take some clubs (you'll need your lob and pitching wedges, for starters) to your backyard so you can teach yourself to hit shots from up against a wall. You'll also need your Fairway Mat (plywood platform covered with SYNLawn synthetic grass) to hit shots from (www.synlawngolf.com), a laundry basket for a target, a "wall-board" (can be a three-foot-long, 2"x 6" piece of lumber) and some almostGOLF balls (www.almostGOLF.com).

Figure 2-16: A few learning aids and you're ready to get started.

You're going to hit shots both ways from against the wall-board on your SYNLawn platform. The wall-board works well because it's heavy enough to stand on its edge to simulate a wall, rock, or tree, yet simple to move when you want to hit from the opposite side of the ball. If your wall-board or platform is not stable enough, put a sandbag or something similar behind or under it to keep it from moving. Aim the wall-board straight ahead to guide your swing path, and place the target basket off to your right in your yard (see Figure 2-17). Then set an almostGOLF ball 3 inches from the wall-board and notice how your normal stance and swing will not work for this shot. But as you address the shot from the left-handed side, and turn your pitching wedge upside down, you are ready to experience this shot for the first time. You're ready to feel and learn the shot from up against the wall!

Figure 2-17: A three-foot-long, 2" x 6" board serves as Eddie's wall-board for his backyard practice.

Now hit twenty-four short shots with your upside-down pitching wedge. This will allow you to launch your shots toward the target basket using a left-handed swing. Carefully aim your clubface before every shot so it looks straight along the direction you want to fly your shot.

Start with small left-handed swings using your pitching wedge. You'll progress up to half-swings and longer with your left-handed motion later. For now, with the target only 10 yards away, begin with just small swings. Your first assignment is to hit twenty-four left-handed shots to your target basket. Please don't try this drill at first with real golf balls. When learning any new shot in your backyard, always start by using almostGOLF balls. They're perfect for practicing shots you're unfamiliar with, because they launch and carry the same as real balls for short distances, but you don't have to worry about denting, breaking or destroying things.

Remember the Launch Direction Rule: Your ball will fly in a direction almost perpendicular to the clubface at impact, regardless of what direction your clubhead swing path is traveling on through impact (in this drill, the swing path is parallel to the wall-board).

LAUNCH RIGHT-HANDED SHOTS

You may have hit a few successful shots from up against the wall-board with your left-handed swings, but don't worry if you haven't, or if it still feels strange. Ideally, you should have noticed that your pitching-wedge shots lofted nicely into the air. Now pick up your wall-board and move it to the other side of the platform tee.

Attempt twenty-four shots from the other side of the wall-board, swinging right-handed but with a very closed clubface (Figure 2-18). Remember to move your target basket again, this time off to the left of your swing line (wall-board) direction. You will immediately notice that with your closed-face pitching-wedge

Figure 2-18: Eddie switches to a wall-board on the right side of the ball.

swing, the ball launches lower than normal off the clubface. This means that on the golf course, it will not only launch low, but will also have almost no backspin. It will roll much farther than most normal pitch shots. Make the switch to your L-wedge and see if you like the trajectory better.

PLAY TO YOUR TARGET

The purpose of this first practice session (forty-eight shots) is to move your intellectual understanding of the Launch Direction Rule into your physical experience. The objective of this first session is to internalize that understanding into your brain and body, never to be forgotten again.

In your second forty-eight-shot session, the objective is to learn how to make against-the-wall swings in varying directions. Once you learn how to aim your clubface, know where and how the shot will fly, and can create consistently solid contact, you're on your way to "owning" this shot.

In your third session (again forty-eight shots, about thirty minutes of practice time), you will need to start paying close attention to how far your shots are carrying in the air. Move your target basket to a different location about every twenty-four shots and see how well you can control the flight of each ball toward your target basket. Try to entice family members or friends to compete with you in these sessions. They'll be a lot more fun and more beneficial to your learning process because competition sharpens your focus.

SWITCH TO REAL GOLF BALLS

Practicing this shot with almostGOLF balls will help you to learn this swing more quickly than if you use real balls, because they're much lighter than normal balls and easier to loft into the air. But once you feel comfortable with your against-the-wall swings, you'll need to start practicing with real golf balls.

When you use real balls in a practice session (again, forty-eight shots), **I recommend you do it on a practice range at a real golf course.** If you try it at home, keep the target basket close to your tee and don't hit shots that are any longer than 10 yards. This way you can practice real-ball sessions to short (less than 10-yard) targets as often as you like in your backyard, and to as many directions as your space will allow. BUT BE CAREFUL: *Real golf balls are a lot harder than almostGOLF balls and can do real damage to neighboring people, windows, and automobiles! Practice with real balls at your own risk!*

TAKE IT TO THE COURSE

Once you take your clubs and wall-board to your golf course practice range, you can hit to various targets on the range from either side of the wall-board. (CAUTION: Always place the ball near the center of the wall-board. Never try to hit a shot from either end of the wall-board, because if you were to swing and hit the end of the board, you could hurt your hands or wrists, or break the club shaft.)

Once you start hitting real balls on the range, it won't be long before you feel confident enough to actually use the against-the-wall shot if you face it on the golf course. You'll be confident with your newfound knowledge of the Launch Direction Rule, not to mention your improved ability to swing and control your clubface angle through impact. You'll find yourself almost looking for these shots on the course, instead of fearing them!

CHAPTER 8

Most Feared Shot #8: The Greenside Pitch

The Shot

WHAT DO YOU SEE IN the photograph in Figure 3-1? If you look at it and think, "What a gorgeous little 30-yard pitch shot," or, "Wow, that waterfall is really nice," then you're okay—you're seeing the game the way it was meant to be enjoyed. If, however, your reaction is, "Oh my God, I could really screw that shot up," then you're thinking like the many golfers who voted the greenside pitch shot as the eighth most feared shot in golf.

Figure 3-1: A 30-yard pitch shot in a gorgeous setting at Atunyote Golf Club, Verona, N.Y.

Now look at Figures 3-2 and 3-3 and tell me what reaction you have to these two situations. Again, some readers might express thoughts of beauty, while others will react with anxiety and fear because of their propensity to hit pitch shots into the trouble they're seeing in front of them.

Figure 3-2: A 15-yard pitch to a beautiful green at Pinehurst No. 2.

Figure 3-3: A longer pitch shot over lots of sand at the Black Course at Bethpage State Park.

Now, I want you to reevaluate these three photographs for a moment and see if you notice something they all have in common. These are typical scenes that we get to enjoy on beautiful golf courses, one of the wonderful parts about this game we love. But they're also typical views that we see before we hit an approach shot—that is, they are full of trouble and bad consequences if we don't execute the shot well.

It's a common phenomenon with short-game shots: The trouble is close to you, right in your face, and it's very distracting. In many instances, it appears there are more trouble areas than safe areas in which to land your golf ball.

The Problem

One of the reasons you fear greenside pitch shots is that you've probably hit the turf behind your ball on a number of occasions, flubbing the shot into the very trouble you're trying to avoid. And when that trouble is so obvious (in other words, right there in front of you), and your shot looks so simple (it just requires a little flip swing), it's embarrassing when you can't pitch it onto the green (Figure 3-4).

Figure 3-4 and inset: A fat greenside pitch shot finds the sand.

Of course, the next time you face a similar shot, you don't want to repeat the same mistake again, so you do everything possible to avoid hitting it fat. You succeed in not hitting it fat, but this time you skull the shot (Figure 3-5).

Figure 3-5 and inset: The skull that follows the fat shot.

The fear of greenside pitch shots doesn't always arise solely from a player's inability to execute a good pitch swing. Sometimes fellow golfers offer advice, suggesting that you "forget about swing mechanics and focus on seeing the shot fly to your target." This often makes matters worse, because everything around your target seems to offer some sort of trouble and possible bad consequences. Other popular advice comes in the opposite form: "Forget about the trouble and bad consequences—just think about your swing mechanics; just think about the process of swinging." But this too often doesn't help either, because many golfers don't know how to execute the mechanics of a proper wedge swing, nor do they know what the proper swing process is supposed to be.

THE CORE OF THE PROBLEM

The core of this problem seems to be that many golfers don't have good pitch swings to start with and don't know what they're doing wrong. As a result, they begin to notice (and pay increased attention to) the trouble surrounding their targets. Anxiety starts to creep into their pre-swing thinking, their adrenaline starts to flow, their muscles get tighter, and their rhythm and mechanics get worse. They wind up hitting worse-than-normal shots that wind up in trouble. The snowball starts rolling, the anxiety begins to spread, and the golfer's problem with pitching grows into a fear of the shot.

Section 3-1: How the Fear of Pitching Develops

1. Tightness creates deceleration in the pitching swing.
2. Anxiety and stress degrade swing rhythm.
3. Tension causes the arms and hands to lose touch.
4. There is no reference, no mind's-eye vision or feel to fall back on.
5. Then, to top it all off, embarrassment often sets in and makes everything worse.

If you have had any of this happen to you, you know how crippling the process can be to your game. Lofting pitch shots onto greens is one of the most frequently needed and important skills in golf, and losing your ability to perform in this area can be devastating.

SOLVING THE PROBLEM BY YOURSELF
DOESN'T WORK

Trying to forget about a fear of pitch shots by simply playing doesn't work. The problem doesn't just go away. Every time you've stayed positive and pretended there's no problem, you've scored horribly. And when you focused on "just making good swings," that didn't work either. You've heard the pros talk about using a swing key, or a thought that they can use to focus on or distract the mind from forming negative thoughts as they swing, but you don't have any of these. And when you try to make one up, it only seems to open the door for more trouble.

You try to control your swing with your hands (what else is there to control it with?), but you see no improvement.

A FEW SKILLS ARE ALL YOU NEED

The good news is that the greenside pitch shot is not an extremely difficult swing move to develop. It doesn't require unusual physical talent, strength, speed, or flexibility. It doesn't even require extreme precision. It simply requires that you develop the following skill set:

1. **Knowledge:** You need to understand (intellectually) what a good pitch swing entails.
2. **Feel:** You need to internalize how it feels to make a proper pitch swing.
3. **Confidence:** You need to build confidence by experiencing good swings and seeing good results.
4. **Swing Memory:** Once you learn the why and how of pitching, you must groove the swing into memory.
5. **Repetition:** The more you practice doing it well, the easier the next shot will become.

The Solution

It's important for you to understand that there is a process for learning how to execute good pitch shots. Solving your pitching problem will take time and practice, but it won't be that difficult. Our five-step solution is as follows:

A FIVE-STEP SOLUTION TO BETTER PITCH SHOTS:

1. Create a mental picture of a "reference" pitching swing in your mind's eye.
2. Calibrate your reference swing for carry distance.
3. Based on variations from your reference swing, groove a "feel for distance" into your mind and muscle memory.
4. Learn how to read what your shots will do after they land on the green.
5. Commit your pitching-swing motion to memory and make it a habit.

FIRST, BUILD A REFERENCE PITCHING SWING

The goal here is to create the knowledge, understanding, and a vision of exactly what you should do and feel to make a good reference pitching swing. You will start this by learning to create one reference swing of a certain size and rhythm, which will be the basis upon which you can then build a complete pitching game. We will show you the positions you need to move through, and the rhythm you need to move in, to create such a swing. This may sound easy, and it is. But without this knowledge, all other efforts you try may be wasted.

You need to form a solid foundation of *knowing* what you're going to do before you spend a large effort trying to do it. You will learn to start, move through, and finish a pitching swing that will stay with you forever (your reference swing), encompassing the three positions shown in Figure 3-6.

Figure 3-6: Three positions of the reference pitch swing.

There will be a number of drills and exercises to help you learn these positions and your reference-swing motion. Those will all be detailed later in the conditioning section.

At this point, you may ask why I chose the swing shown above as your reference swing. The reason is that this swing is easy to execute and remember (it has certain characteristic positions that your brain and body can recognize/repeat), and it is also the most common pitching swing that golfers need when they miss greens. It's one of the swings you'll need most in your golf career, and it's important that you learn to play it with accuracy and consistency.

CALIBRATE YOUR REFERENCE-SWING DISTANCE

After you build a reference swing that you can repeat, you have to determine how far it carries the ball. When you're on the golf course and need a different distance, you'll have a known reference swing that you can adjust up or down from (by making a longer or shorter swing), to produce the carry distance you need. And when you need a shot that will carry exactly your reference-swing yardage, you'll have that one down *cold*.

GROOVE A FEEL FOR DISTANCE INTO YOUR MIND AND MUSCLE MEMORY

Once you know your basic swing and how far it flies the ball, you'll start to develop a feel for making swings that carry shots different distances. Using different target distances in structured practice sessions, you can develop this feel in a reasonable amount of time. During your distance drills you will incorporate the habit of making a serious practice swing (to feel the right swing for the distance you need) before every shot.

LEARN TO READ WHAT YOUR PITCH SHOTS WILL DO AFTER THEY LAND ON GREENS

Once you can execute your pitching swing properly and repeatedly, you're halfway home in your quest to remove your fear of this shot. That's because launching a pitch shot is only the first half of executing one successfully. You also need to learn how the shot will react in terms of trajectory, backspin, roll, and stopping distance on the greens. This "second half" of pitching can only be done while pitching to real holes on real greens (or SYNLawn greens in your backyard).

COMMIT YOUR PITCHING SWING TO MEMORY AND MAKE IT A HABIT

Finally, you must commit to "doing your job" on the golf course. It's vital that you understand this concept, because your job on the golf course is to choose the right shot and then execute it to the best of your ability. You have no other responsibility. You can't control the wind, bad bounces, unseen conditions that may exist, or the wrath of the "Golf Gods," which *will* descend upon you from time to time. You can, however, control which shots you choose to play, as well as the length and rhythm of the swings you make. This and this alone is your responsibility. Choose your shot, select your landing area, and make the best swing you can. You do your job and let the rest of the game be what it may.

How It Should Look

I don't want everyone's pitching swing to look like mine, like a particular PGA TOUR pro's, or like anyone else's but yours. Everyone signs their name differently, everyone has a different set of fingerprints, and everyone swings their golf club in a slightly different rhythm and style. So don't think that any one look or position is exactly how *you* should look.

Nevertheless, the fundamentals for hitting a solid pitch shot are the same for every player. Two of these fundamentals are 1) you must deliver your wedge to the ball cleanly, without getting dirt or grass between the clubface and the ball, and 2) the clubhead must accelerate through impact, to minimize any errors caused by an off-sweet-spot hit.

Beyond that, a comfortable stance width—aligned either at the target or slightly open to it (to the left for right-handed players), with the ball positioned within an inch of center in the stance (Figure 3-7)—should be sufficient to launch a solid pitch shot. There doesn't need to be anything special about your grip, except that if your grip is too strong (with your right hand too far under the shaft) or too tight, you'll struggle when you try to hit high shots.

Figure 3-7 and inset: My setup and grip for a 30-yard pitch shot.

One of the biggest fear-inducing aspects of the greenside pitch shot is that when you look at your target, you frequently see trouble (Figure 3-8)—lots of trouble. In reality of course, if you make a good pitch swing, it won't matter what lies between your ball and your target landing area, because your ball will fly over it. Just remember, when you look up at address after determining your ball and feet positions, your focus should be on your target and the swing size you'll need to get your ball there. And your mind's eye should be focused on correlating the size of your pitching swing (swing length) with your desired carry distance—nothing else.

Figure 3-8: A Golfer's-Eye View of a beautiful yet possibly scary 30-yard pitch shot over water.

The key to executing a solid pitch shot is to internalize and habitualize your pitching-swing motion. Once you're able to execute your swing out of habit—without thinking about it—your mind can focus on how long your swing needs to be to fly the ball to your intended landing area.

For a 30-yard pitch, my backswing has to be a little longer than my reference backswing (which flies my ball 15 yards). I make several practice swings (true rehearsals, looking up at the target after each swing), until I feel that my backswing is the right length for the shot distance at hand. Then I step up to my ball, take one look at the target, waggle the clubhead, and swing (Figure 3-9). If you look carefully, you can see that my wedge kicked up a small tuft of grass on this shot. Your pitching swing shouldn't create divots from 15 yards, but at around 30 or 40 yards you should begin taking divots instead of having the sole of your wedge just "kiss" and bounce off the turf.

Figure 3-9: My downswing and through-swing for a 30-yard pitch shot.

The more I play this game, the more I appreciate its beauty and wonder. And it's surprising how this simple motion is responsible for one of the most feared shots in the game. I hope you can see now that it really isn't that complex a motion, especially when you compare it to hitting a 270-yard drive down the center of the fairway. Now *that's* a difficult swing to execute!

By making a nice, smooth swing motion from the top of your backswing and accelerating the club through to the finish (keeping your body and club moving together), you can produce one of the most beautiful and poetic ball flights in the game (Figure 3-10).

Figure 3-10: My incoming 30-yard pitch shot.

Figure 3-11:
Fred Couples
has some of
the softest
hands in the
business.

Now, if you would like to see something a lot more poetic than my swing, watch the pitching swing motion of Fred Couples. No one swings the club more rhythmically and with softer hands than Freddie does (Figure 3-11). When you see his swing motion in real time, it's a gentle rhythm—a lot more swinging through the ball than hitting at the ball. Of course, Freddie's rhythmic full golf swing is legendary, but I feel that his short-game rhythm is also a real strength of his game. Freddie just lets the ball get in the way of his gentle, rhythmic, beautiful wedge swing.

Another player with great rhythm is Phil Mickelson. Widely considered to be the best short-game player ever, Phil's pitching motion is beautiful to behold (Figure 3-12, reversed to show him swinging right-handed). The more you look at Couples's and Mickelson's pitching motions, the better your own pitching swings will become. The brain has a way of learning through osmosis, so let it feast on these two examples and absorb as much as it can.

Figure 3-12: Phil Mickelson's pitching swing reversed to appear right-handed.

Additional Shots

One can take the fundamentals of the reference pitch swing (Figure 3-13) and apply them to longer wedge shots. By swinging the club back and through a little farther, you can stretch this shot out to longer (Figure 3-14) and longer (Figure 3-15) distances.

Figure 3-13: The reference pitch backswing position.

Figure 3-14: As the length of the swing increases, the carry length of the shot increases.

And if you want to see beauty in motion, watch major-championship winner Steve Elkington hit a 15-yard pitch shot at Colonial Country Club in Fort Worth, Texas (Figure 3-16). It just doesn't get any better than this, and he makes it look so easy.

Figure 3-15: My pitching swing can play safely to the middle of this green.

Figure 3-16: The perfect pitching technique of Steve Elkington.

Success Examples

By now, I hope I've convinced you that the pitching swing is not among the most difficult swings in golf to execute. Once you learn the mechanics of a simple reference pitch swing, and then get some good rhythm and practice swings behind you, you'll be able to master this part of your short game.

Having said this, however, I don't want you to think that after hitting one or two really good shots, you've "got it" for the rest of your playing days. Any golf shot that requires as much feel, rhythm, and timing in its execution as the greenside pitch, will always take a lot of practice to remain dialed-in. Lots of small muscles in your feet, knees, core, and shoulders help to keep your balance and execution just right to create the shots you want. All LPGA and PGA TOUR professionals, including the likes of Phil Mickelson (Figure 3-17), spend a significant amount of practice time fine-tuning their pitching games around the greens.

Figure 3-17: Phil Mickelson at the 2006 Open Championship.

Figure 3-18: Phil's short game isn't luck. He works on it.

Mickelson changes his lie and incoming angle to the pin slightly when practicing his pitching technique (Figure 3-18), then goes for another bucket of balls.

Then he changes to yet another pitch-shot angle (Figure 3-19) and repeats the process again. Have you heard that he has "oodles" of talent? He does, but he also spends lots of time fine-tuning it.

Figure 3-19: Mickelson continues to hone his pitch swing at the Open Championship.

Figure 3-20: Lefty practicing to a towel positioned 30 yards away.

Sometimes it's easier to practice your distance control to a towel (Figure 3-20) or a laundry basket. This is great practice, because once you can land your ball in the target area you've chosen on the course, you also find it rolling up and stopping close to the flagstick.

Every fairway, green, and hole is different. The slopes are different, the terrain is different, and, of course, weather conditions can change the whole ballgame overnight. So even after you've learned how to pitch the ball accurately and have replaced the fear you had with confidence on these shots, it will still take consistent, relentless practice to keep your pitch shots hunting the hole (Figure 3-21).

Figure 3-21: Mickelson pitching to a flagstick during a practice round at the 2009 U.S. Open at Bethpage Black.

I want to remind you that even the pros aren't always successful in pitching their shots close to the pin. Sometimes golfers are so hard on themselves that they forget that the simpler shots in golf are still very easy to mess up. As proof of this, I spent an entire golf season at various PGA TOUR venues for the Golf Channel, replicating the short-game shots that players didn't quite pull off during that particular tournament (Figure 3-22).

Figure 3-22: Re-creating a 30-yard pitch to the 18th green at TPC Sawgrass for the Golf Channel.

Conditioning Process

I hope that by now you believe you can beat your fear of the greenside pitch shot. If so, it's time to get to work. Let's start by reviewing the list of the things you need to accomplish to become good at pitching the golf ball.

Section 3-2: To conquer your fear of the pitch shot:

IN YOUR BACKYARD

1. Create a vision in your mind's eye and a feel in your body for your reference pitching swing.
2. Groove your reference swing (without using a ball).
3. Calibrate the carry distance of your reference pitch shot with almostGOLF balls.
4. Practice to different distances to help create your feel for distance.
5. Commit your pitching swing to memory (i.e., make it a habit).

AT THE GOLF COURSE

1. Learn your shot distances with real golf balls and how they react on the green.
2. Practice doing your job.

CREATE THE REFERENCE SWING

Start this process at home. After studying the positions you want to replicate at the top of your backswing and finish, you can learn to make a reference pitching swing indoors in the comfort of your garage or den (you should need only an eight-foot-high ceiling to swing under).

Now I want to show you exactly what constitutes a perfect reference swing. You need to understand the details of this swing motion so that you can internalize its feel and commit it to muscle memory. Please don't misinterpret what we're doing here: I want you to understand what your perfect pitch swing looks and feels like so you can learn it, feel it, own it, and then forget about it. I'm not going to teach you to think your way through your pitch swing. That's not what you want to do. Instead, I'm going to have you first understand it, and then learn it well enough so that it automatically comes out of memory as a habit, without thinking about it, when you use it.

Carefully examine Figure 3-23, which demonstrates the top of the backswing position for the reference pitch swing. At this point, your hands should be midway between your knees and waist, with your wrists cocked 90 degrees. The back of your left hand should face straight away from you, perpendicular to the plane of your swing.

Next, see the perfect position for the finish of the reference swing (Figure 3-24). At the end of your follow-through, the back of your left hand and clubface should face in the opposite direction, again perpendicular to your swing plane but this time facing behind you. Your hands should be just above waist high, with the wedge shaft vertical.

Figure 3-23: Top of the backswing position for the reference pitch swing.

Figure 3-24: The finish position for the reference pitch swing.

Figure 3-25: My reference pitch swing in full motion.

Having seen both ends of the swing, I want you to recognize that the heart of your reference swing will be the smooth, accelerating swing action that connects the top of your backswing to your finish (Figure 3-25). It involves no golf ball, and there is no hit or force applied by your hands through impact. You use your hands only to hold on to the club in this smooth and rhythmic motion.

KISS THE GRASS

This may surprise you, but the reference pitch swing should leave no divot. The bottom (sole) of your wedge should only kiss or brush the ground beneath the ball, leaving a small mark on the grass or dirt (Figure 3-26).

Figure 3-26: A close-up of impact with the clubhead brushing the ground: there should be no divot.

SWING RHYTHM

There is no one set rhythm or pace that applies to all golfers. But there is a natural, smooth, accelerating rhythm that applies and is unique to every golfer. After working with thousands of students in our schools on their pitching swings, our instructors have found that if you say the two words "saaaawish" and "swish," you will have timed the rhythm of your backswing and forward swing, as shown in Figure 3-27.

Figure 3-27: Backswing rhythm: Saaaawish.

Your backswing should be slower and take slightly more time, as if to the rhythm of your saying the word "saaaawish."

Then your down and through swing should be faster and more aggressive and take less time, as if to the rhythm of your saying the word "swish."

Once you learn to get your hands, arms, and club into the perfect reference backswing and follow-through positions, and your club is swinging along the proper path through impact, about the only thing left for you to worry about is your swing rhythm.

Figure 3-27: Down-and-through swing rhythm: Swish.

IF YOU'RE HAVING TROUBLE

In our schools we've found that the action of making an underhanded toss with a heavy medicine ball (don't do this if you have a bad back) creates the same feel and motion of a good pitching swing (compare Figure 3-28 with Figure 3-25 earlier). A heavy medicine ball weighs about eight pounds. If you pinch both elbows into your sides as you hold the ball at address, then gently swing it back and through (keep your elbows pinched), tossing it about three feet as you follow through (Figure 3-28), you should get the feel of the correct body motion for your pitching swing.

STRENGTHEN YOUR LEFT SIDE WITH THE LEFT-ARM-ONLY DRILL

For golfers who don't have complete control of their wedge swings, I suggest the left-arm-only drill (Figure 3-29). Start by taking your normal address position (again with no golf ball), then remove your right hand from the club and stick it in your right pocket. Tuck your right elbow into your right side and make your reference pitch swing with your left arm only.

If you're not strong enough to make this swing motion, you need to continue to practice this drill. This will strengthen your forearms and wrists over time and help you gain better control of your wedge swings. This drill also helps you feel the rhythm of your body turn. Once you're able to make a reasonable left-arm-only swing, you'll find that you have more control over your two-handed reference swing.

Figure 3-29:
Left-arm-only
swing.

GROOVE YOUR REFERENCE SWING

One more drill before the fun starts. Spend ten minutes a day for one week making perfect reference pitch swings in your backyard. Don't hit balls yet. It's better that you don't worry about where the ball goes after each swing. Instead, concentrate on swinging in good rhythm and getting your back- and through-swing positions correct. Your swing path through impact should run along the target line, and your clubhead should brush the grass, not dig into it. Actually say to yourself "saaaawish" on your backswing and "swish" on your follow-through during each swing.

In each ten-minute session you'll make about a hundred swings. Quality, not quantity, is key here. If you don't feel comfortable that you're making really good pitch swings after a week, then take another week, or two repeating the drill.

CALIBRATE THE CARRY DISTANCE OF YOUR REFERENCE PITCH SWING WITH ALMOSTGOLF BALLS

When you feel good about your swing action, go get some almostGOLF balls and set up on your hitting platform. Hit twenty-four balls with the best reference swings you can make, and don't worry about the outcome—just try to repeat the reference swing. Now take a marker (a pylon, in my case, but a tennis ball or basketball will do nicely) and place it in the center of your shot pattern. Measure the distance from the center of your shot pattern back to your hitting platform—this is the average distance that your reference pitch swing sends the almostGOLF balls.

Repeat one twenty-four-shot pattern every day for seven days and see how consistently your distance repeats. If your average reference-swing distance varies day to day by more than 5 yards, continue this drill until you get its variation to within 2 yards. Then take another week to repeat the same process, but this time use real balls. They'll fly almost the same distance on these short shots, but you'll want to accurately measure the distance they fly anyway. The important thing is to know whether your reference pitch shot travels 14, 15, or maybe 17 yards (or whatever). Remember, every golfer is different, and you need to know how far, on average, *your* reference pitch swing flies *your* pitch shots.

DEVELOP A FEEL FOR DISTANCE

Now it's time for some drills that will help you to learn how to hit pitch shots to a variety of distances. The length of your swing determines the carry distance of your shot (Figure 3-30). The farther you want to carry the ball, the longer you swing both back and through. Short swings create short shots, long swings produce long shots. This concept makes it easy to learn distance control.

OPPOSITE: Figure 3-30: Short swings for short shots, long swings for long shots. (A = reference swing, B = longer swing, C = shorter swing)

3-30A.1

3-30A.2

3-30B.1

3-30B.2

3-30C.1

3-30C.2

PRACTICE DIFFERENT DISTANCES

From your backyard SYNLawn platform, with almostGOLF balls and a laundry basket for your target, you're ready to start grooving your reference swing (Figure 3-31). Your drill is to pitch forty-eight shots per session, three times a week for two months.

You will want to move your target basket after each twenty-four-shot session to keep your focus on hitting shots the correct distance. At least once a week, make sure to check that the target basket is at your exact reference-swing distance (which should produce your most accurate shot pattern). In two months, you will have hit more than a thousand shots, gaining confidence in your pitching ability with each session.

As you start these sessions, also make it a habit to rehearse your swing before each shot. Make this practice swing a real

Figure 3-31: Backyard setup to a target basket.

attempt to create the right swing length for the distance you desire, and don't forget to make it a swing motion that brushes the turf in a "saaaawish–swish" rhythm. Over time your feel for distance will become automatic, leading to precise pitch shots when you get to the golf course.

Your backyard pitching drills can go on for as long as you like, but to become really good you must hit at least several thousand shots. Don't let that number scare you, because you can hit a hundred balls in one session in your backyard in about thirty minutes (Figure 3-32). If you do this for twenty or thirty sessions, you'll start to internalize and own a good pitching-swing motion. After all, that's what this training is about.

Figure 3-32: Commit your pitch swing to memory with lots of practice sessions.

TAKE IT TO THE COURSE

Figure 3-33: The T-Square helps with your alignment and ball position.

Now you're ready to take your improved pitching motion to the golf course. Go to the short-game practice area with an ample supply of balls and an alignment aid called the T-Square (Figure 3-33). The main rod of the T-Square should aim at your target, while the perpendicular rod will help you develop a consistent ball position in the middle of your stance.

Start by brushing the grass on your shorter pitch shots (under 30 yards). These brush marks will turn into divots (Figure 3-34) when your swing gets longer and you have to hit the ball farther, beginning around 40 yards or more.

You can hit seven shots from one position using the T-Square before you must move to a new patch of turf and reset it (Figure 3-35).

Figure 3-34: Divots should begin on the target side of your original ball position.

Figure 3-35: Hit seven shots from a perfectly aligned position, then move to a new location and start over.

Before you start your practice, find the best green available. It should be one that provides ample feedback on how your shots will react when they land on the green (Figure 3-36).

Figure 3-36: Your practice green should provide you with feedback on how the ball will react when it lands.

I recommend that after every few shots you back off and re-start again from behind your ball. Then walk into the shot as you would on the golf course (Figure 3-37).

Figure 3-37: Just like you would on the course, start from behind the ball and visualize the perfect shot in your mind's eye.

When practicing, most golfers get sloppy and don't rehearse properly. Don't make this mistake. Take at least one practice swing to feel the right swing length before every shot. Don't rush or take too much time over the ball. Practice at the same rhythm you use to address and hit shots on the course (Figure 3-38).

Don't always practice from perfect fairway lies. You'll hit more pitch shots from the rough than you will from the fairway over a season of golf (Figure 3-39). But all the same rules for the pitching-swing motion apply, except when the ball is sitting down in the rough. In this instance, you should begin to move your ball position farther back in your stance to create a more descending strike and catch less grass between the ball and the clubface.

Figure 3-38: Practice the way you play, using the same rhythm you use to hit shots on the course.

Figure 3-39: Practice from the rough as much as you do from fairway lies.

And there you have it. This time next year you'll be saying: "I'm so proud—I can hit pitch shots with confidence and not worry about bad consequences. I'm so glad I took the time to develop my reference pitch swing because I can hit the ball to any distance. I love to pitch the ball now!"

Most Feared Shot #7:
Hitting Through Trees

The Shot

THE REASON THIS SHOT (FIGURE 4-1) is feared by so many golfers is clear: The odds of success are low, and the consequences of failure can be severe in terms of damage to your score. Golfers facing this situation usually set up by aiming between the trees, unaware that even a perfectly struck shot might well hit the tree on one side or the other of their target line. The reason for this is that very few players, including PGA TOUR pros, hit shots that fly in a dead-straight direction.

One of the more difficult things to do in golf is to control the trajectory of a shot. As you can see in Figure 4-1, there is an opening directly in line with the flagstick. But aiming at the flagstick would be dangerous and probably not in my best interest, because if I try the shot and hit it on a slightly imperfect trajectory, the ball could hit either tree and bounce who knows where. With out-of-bounds on the right, I wouldn't want to chance that happening.

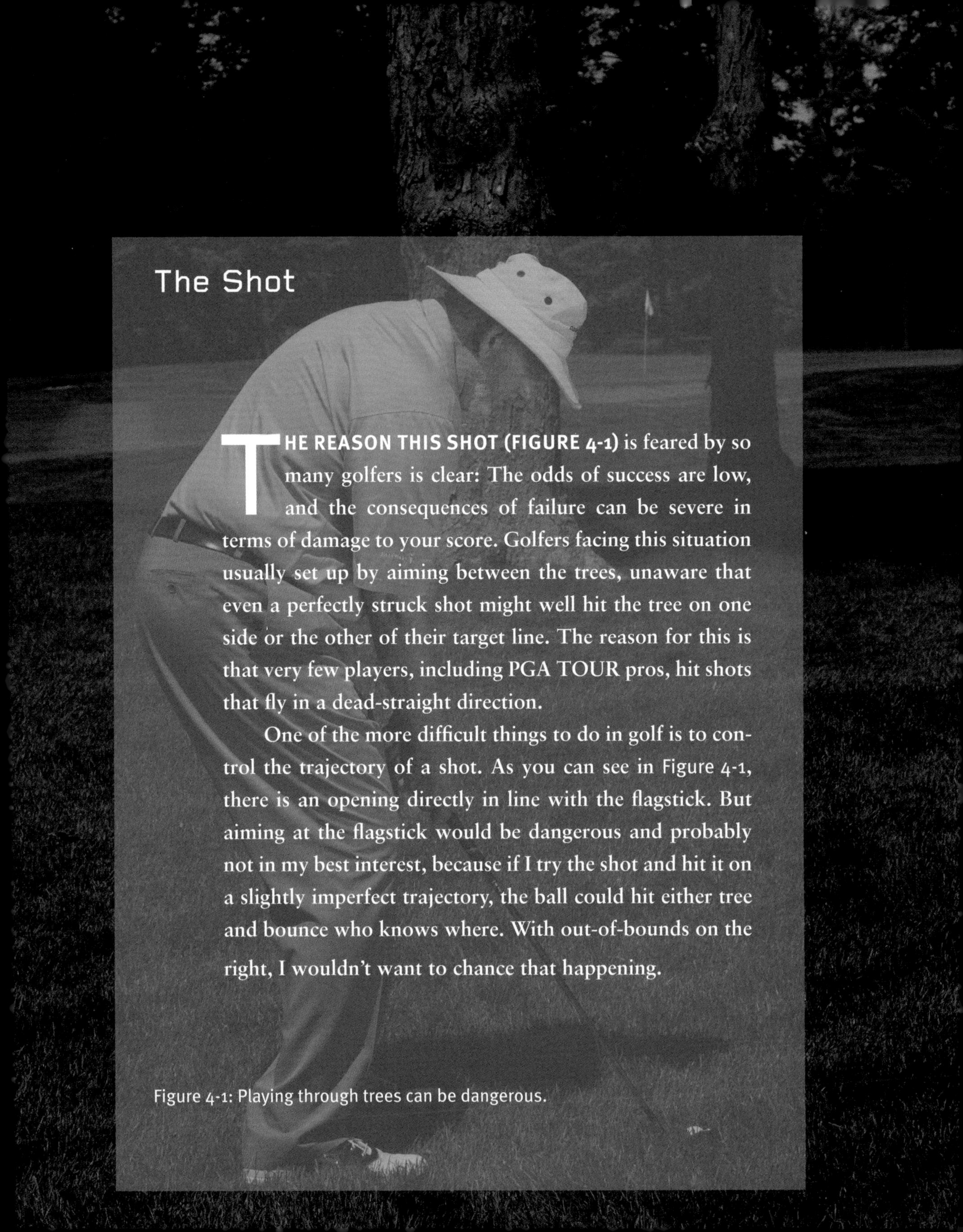

Figure 4-1: Playing through trees can be dangerous.

The Problem

Every year for the past ten years, I have accompanied a research team from the Pelz Golf Institute to the World Amateur Handicap Championship to study how amateurs play the game. This five-day competition in Myrtle Beach, South Carolina, annually features 4,000-plus serious amateur golfers playing more than sixty quality golf courses each day for the first four days (only flight winners play the last day). For the last three years our team has included the PGA TOUR's ShotLink staff and their laser-based data-collection system.

In our most feared shot survey, we discovered that amateurs fear hitting through trees, but don't try or even think about trying to curve shots around them. In our Myrtle Beach research, we confirmed that they have many opportunities to attempt hitting shots between trees, and frequently pay the price for trying to do so.

The difficulty with hitting shots between trees is that it requires one to start the ball precisely on line and keep it on that line without curving the ball in either direction: a very daunting task. More often than not, the results are undesirable (Figure 4-2).

Figure 4-2: A World Amateur contestant tries unsuccessfully to hit between trees.

Both golf balls and tree trunks are fairly hard objects. When two hard objects meet, and one is moving at a high speed while the other is massive and immovable, crazy bounces ensue. A very practical tip for all golfers is to avoid hitting objects like trees, especially when they are close to you, because your ball can bounce into really bad situations (for example, out of bounds).

This is easier said than done, however, because most golfers hit shots with either a slight fade or draw trajectory, and don't always play for their off-line curvature when they pick targets as they try to escape from trouble (in other words, they don't really know where to aim). Many others play the game with either big slices or hooks, which makes this problem even worse. Most golfers think that when they successfully hit a shot to their target, their ball flew straight there. In fact, most shots curve in one direction or the other on their way to wherever they land, and almost nobody achieves straight-line trajectory shots on a consistent basis.

The Solution

To avoid hitting trees, bushes, or whatever obstacles are in your way on the golf course, the solution is not to attempt shots between them, through them, or even close to them. It is a far better solution to learn to generously curve your shots around them, with plenty of room to spare. Here's how:

1. Learn the three laws of ball flight and how a ball comes off the clubface.
2. Learn how to set up and aim your body, your swing path direction, and your clubface to control the direction and curvature of your shots.

The great thing about this solution is that you can achieve it using your normal swing, which you already know how to do.

To see how a ball reacts after impact with a golf club, examine the ball-flight laws (Section 4-1) and diagrams (Figure 4-3) that follow. Study them until you completely understand how the face angle and swing path determine the curvature of shots.

Section 4-1: The Laws of Ball Flight

LAW #1. Golf balls launch in a direction essentially perpendicular to the clubface at impact.

LAW #2. Balls curve in the direction the clubface is aimed relative to the clubhead's swing path through impact.

LAW #3. The amount of shot curvature is controlled by the difference between the clubhead swing path direction and the aim direction of the clubface at impact—the more separation there is between the two, the greater the degree of curvature.

Balls launch to the right and slice farther to the right when the face is aimed to the right of the club's swing path at impact. Balls launch to the left—and hook farther to the left—when the face is aimed left of the club's swing path at impact. The only shots that fly straight are the ones hit by a clubface that is perfectly square to the clubhead path at impact.

It's much easier to grasp these three laws in pictures. Study Figure 4-3 to understand the initial launch direction and curvature of a ball's flight relative to the swing path of a golf club and the aim direction of its clubface at impact.

Notice that balls launch in a direction perpendicular to the clubface, no matter if the face is aimed to the right (open) or to the left (closed) of the club's swing path through impact. Also note how the ball will curve still farther away from the clubhead's swing path in whichever direction the face is aimed at impact.

Please make sure you understand these fundamentals of launch direction and curvature before proceeding from here. If you don't, your intuition for curving shots around trees on the golf course will

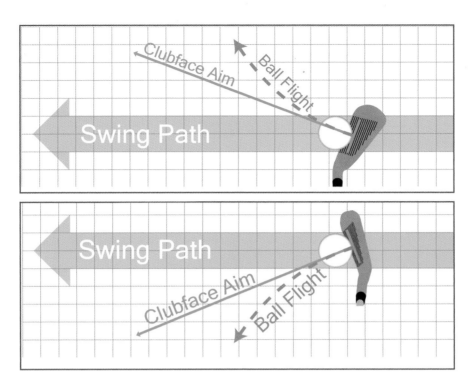

Figure 4-3: A shot's launch direction and in-flight curvature is determined by the club's swing path and face angle (where it's pointing) at impact.

be seriously hindered. It must make sense to you that if you hit a ball with an open clubface relative to your club's swing's path, your shot (for right-handed golfers) will launch to the right of that swing line and curve even farther to the right. Likewise, if you hit a ball with a closed clubface relative to your club's swing path, the shot will launch to the left of that swing line and curve even farther to the left as it flies.

If you feel like you have a good understanding of the ball-flight laws, then proceed; if not, please take this book (and Figure 4-3 above) to your local PGA golf professional and discuss it. Your intuition as to how to create a slice versus a hook needs to be correct before the rest of this chapter will make sense or help you conquer your fear of this shot.

BODY AND SWING PATH ALIGNMENT VS. CLUBFACE AIM FOR CURVING SHOTS

Once you intellectually understand how and why shots curve, you need to learn how to aim your body and swing in one direction while aiming the clubface in another. This simple skill will enable you to curve your shots.

There are several ways to physically achieve an open or closed clubface at impact in a golf swing. Some golfers, including many pros, do it by using special grips or making different swing motions that they've learned over the years. But there is an easier way. I recommend you create fades, slices, draws, and hooks using your normal everyday golf swing, changing only where your body and swing path are aimed at address, and then how much you open or close your clubface before you swing. This is the simplest way to control where your shots start and how much they curve in flight.

SETUP FOR A FADE/SLICE

To hit a slice, you only have to remember a simple two-step procedure that will govern your setup, alignment, and clubface aim. First determine your body setup and swing direction (the yellow line in Figure 4-4), then regrip and aim the clubface halfway between your swing direction and your target (the white line in Figure 4-4).

THE SLICE RULE (SEE FIGURE 4-4)

1. Set up/aim your body and swing direction (yellow line) 50 yards left of the target.
2. Loosen your grip and rotate the club open to aim the clubface (solid white line) halfway (25 yards left) to the target.
3. Regrip so your hands are in your normal takeaway position while the clubface is still open (aimed halfway back to target).
4. Make your normal swing in the 50-yards-left direction (yellow line).
5. Your ball will launch in a 25-yards-left direction (white line) and slice toward the target (dashed white line).

This means that if you set up and swing in a direction 50 yards left of your target, you open the clubface halfway back (25 yards left) to your target before you swing. You want your clubface to be aimed 25 yards left of the target when it hits the ball, because that's the line

Figure 4-4: To hit an intentional slice, aim way left of your target (yellow line), rotate the clubface halfway back to the target (solid white line), then use your normal swing.

you want your ball to launch on. It will start flying on this line 25 yards left of target, and then slice to the target (dashed white line).

I want to emphasize a point here: When I tell you to aim your body and swing 50 yards to the left, that means you are setting up and making a swing that would normally hit the shot 50 yards to the left of your target—if you kept your clubface square to your swing direction (as you normally would in most golf shots). It means that when you rotate your clubface open to aim halfway to your target (25 yards left of target), you must still swing in the 50-yards-left direction.

In other words, don't swing where you've aimed your clubface; always swing where you've aimed your body *before* you opened the clubface. (Note: When you open the clubface you will also increase the club's loft at impact, and your slice shots will fly higher than normal for whatever club you use. For this shot, I used an open-faced 7-iron to create an 8-iron trajectory.)

Of course, learning exactly how far left to aim and swing when you want to curve a ball to the right around a tree will require a little experimentation on your part. In your own game you will have to learn how your clubface alignment looks versus the result it produces.

How It Should Look

THE SETUP/AIM AND FACE ALIGNMENT FOR A SLICE

Look carefully at my setup and face alignment in Figure 4-5 below. To hit the big intentional slice you saw in Figure 4-4 above, I set up for a three-quarter 7-iron shot and aimed way left (50 yards left) of the green. Next, I adjusted my aim back until it was 25 yards left of the flagstick. To adjust my clubface aim, I relaxed my left-hand grip and rotated the face open with my right hand. I then regripped the club with both hands in their normal address position.

You must regrip your club with your hands in their normal position—exactly the way you have them when you expect to hit a straight shot with a square clubface—while the clubface remains open. Remember, to slice a shot you must have your clubface open relative to your swing path at impact. So when you lay it open, do so by sliding it open **WITHOUT MOVING YOUR HANDS FROM THEIR NORMAL GRIP POSITION** at address. Don't rotate both your club and your hands open. If you rotate your hands to open the clubface, they will just return to their normal position at impact (out of habit), thus squaring your clubface at impact and eliminating any chance you have of slicing the shot.

Figure 4-5: To slice, aim left, rotate the clubface open halfway back to the target, regrip with your hands in the normal grip position, and swing.

Now look down at my feet (right-hand page) in the Golfer's-Eye View image in Figure 4-6. Note how open my clubface is relative to my swing line, which is parallel to my foot line. Imagine you're standing in this position, then rotate the book clockwise 45 degrees and simultaneously tilt your head left and look up at the left-hand page (now on top). This is how the shot would look to you from your address position on the golf course, after you rotated your head up and to the left to look at the target.

Figure 4-6: Golfer's-Eye View
for my slice around two trees.

At this point, try to visualize your own setup for this shot as you rotate the book back and forth. Look at the right-hand page as though you were looking down at your own feet, then rotate the book clockwise and look at the top (left-hand) page to see the target. Now imagine what it would feel like to make your normal golf swing and hit this shot without making any adjustments to your hands or swing. Make your last look along your setup/aim direction, look down at the ball, and make a good three-quarter 7-iron swing. Can you feel the ball slice off your clubface, around the trees, and head directly toward the flagstick (Figure 4-7)?

Figure 4-7: My normal three-quarter 7-iron swing from a slice setup and open-faced alignment.

If you were standing behind the green watching the shot I hit from this slice setup, you would have seen the incoming ball flight shown in Figure 4-8. This was a very simple swing to make: a three-quarter 7-iron swing. Notice how my ball came nowhere close to hitting the trees. It was a very safe shot. Even if I hadn't opened the clubface just the right amount, the shot still would have ended up somewhere around the green with no chance of a collision with either tree.

Figure 4-8: My normal swing motion from an open-faced slice setup easily curves the ball around the trees to my target.

TO HIT DRAWS AND HOOKS, JUST REVERSE THE SLICE RULE

Once you understand the slice rule, all you have to do to hit hooking shots is reverse the directions. Simply aim your body and swing to the right of your target, close your clubface halfway back to your target, regrip so the clubface stays closed through impact, and swing where you aimed your body (to the right). To review the impact fundamentals that produce draws and hooks, refer back to Figure 4-3. And please notice: closing the clubface decreases the club's loft, so to produce an 8-iron trajectory you'll want to use your 9-iron.

LEARN YOUR BODY AND SWING AIM, THEN YOUR CLUBFACE ALIGNMENT FOR A DRAW/HOOK

As in learning to fade and slice shots, knowing how far right to aim for draws and hooks will take practice. But the "Hook Rule" is the same as the "Slice Rule," except in the opposite direction.

THE HOOK RULE (SEE FIGURE 4-9)

1. Set up/aim your body and swing direction (yellow line) X-yards right of the target.

2. Loosen your grip and rotate the clubface closed (white line) halfway back to the target.

3. Regrip the club so your hands are in a normal takeaway position while the clubface remains closed (aimed halfway back to the target).

4. Swing (use your normal swing) at the X-yards-right-of-target direction (yellow line).

5. The ball will launch in a halfway X-yards-right direction (white dash line), draw/hook toward the target, and bounce left toward the target.

You must aim far enough to the right so that when your ball launches in a direction halfway between your swing line and the target, it will then curve around the tree with plenty of margin for error before heading toward the green (Figure 4-9). This means if you aim your body and swing 30 yards right of your target, you should then close your clubface to aim 15 yards right of the target before swinging.

Figure 4-9: To hit an intentional hook, aim your body and swing line right of the target (yellow line), then close the clubface halfway back to your target (white) and swing.

GOOD SETUP/AIM AND FACE ALIGNMENT
FOR HOOKS/DRAWS

Similar to the slice setup procedure, I start my hook setup by positioning my body and club for a straight, three-quarter 9-iron shot. This time, however, I aim my body and swing line 30 yards to the right of the target. Then I relax my grip and rotate my 9-iron clubface closed until it is halfway back to the target. (NOTE: Because the face is shutting down through impact and losing loft, the 9-iron produces an 8-iron trajectory.) Lastly, I regrip my hands into their normal address position (Figure 4-10).

Figure 4-10: Setup for an intentional draw/hook.

From this address position I simply try to make a good swing (Figure 4-11). This hook swing is the same swing I used for the slice shot in Figure 4-7 above, except that the face angle starts closed instead of open, and returns to closed (instead of open) through impact.

Figure 4-11: My normal swing with a closed clubface produces a draw/hook shot.

As you can see, my normal swing motion curves the ball from right to left from my closed-face setup position (Figure 4-12). If you stood behind the green and watched this ball hook in toward the flagstick, you'd see that it never came close to hitting either tree. Again, a very safe shot with plenty of margin for error, using an easy-to-execute swing.

Figure 4-12: Because the clubface is closed through impact and I'm aiming so far to the right, the ball hooks to the left, around the trees.

Success Examples

If you've played the game for any length of time, you probably know the value of being able to curve shots on demand. I'm sure you've tried to bend shots and failed at the cost of one or more strokes, just as you've been successful at other times in saving strokes. The example I would like to show you here is of the best curving slice shot you could ever want to see. It was pulled off by Phil Mickelson at the 2002 U.S. Open, as he played the 13th hole at Bethpage Black golf course. Because it was never on television (NBC didn't have cameras as far off course as he got on that hole), very few people know about it. But the following photographs will show you what happened (Figures 4-14 through 4-17).

In 2002, the 13th hole played as a 545-yard par 5. During the third round, Phil hit a good drive and then went for the green in two with a 4-wood. He hit it well, but it faded some 30 yards left of the green. As he and his caddy "Bones" approached the green, the crowd noise and clamor grew and grew, and they soon learned that the ball had dribbled onto a blacktop maintenance road at the edge of the ropes. It had barely trickled onto the road, but then gained a little speed and rolled into the gutter swale on the side of the road. The problem was, the road sloped downhill, and Phil's ball didn't stop rolling until it came to rest at the bottom of the hill, an additional 140 yards farther to the left of the green. The ball settled in a nursery area where no one was ever supposed to be (except for maintenance people and spectators taking a shortcut through the nursery). I remind you—this all happened during actual play in the U.S. Open, to the man who ended up finishing in second place!

In Figure 4-13, I'm standing as if playing a left-handed shot from where Mickelson's second shot finally came to rest that day. As you can see in the photo, a sign is there to help spectators find their way back to the golf course.

Figure 4-13: Mickelson's second shot on the par-5 13th hole at Bethpage Black (third round, 2002 U.S. Open) finally stopped at the edge of a nursery, 180 yards left of the green.

Figure 4-14: Mickelson's view from the road back up toward the 13th green. Yes, the ball was still in play.

Figure 4-15: Mickelson used a 6-iron to cut his ball up the road to safety.

During the 2009 U.S. Open my son Eddie and I walked down, and he took these pictures to re-create and explain this shot. Figure 4-14 shows the third shot Mickelson faced after his ball had rolled all the way down the road and into the nursery. Can you imagine looking up and seeing this view when you're contending for the U.S. Open Championship?

Well, as you've probably guessed by now, Phil hit a nice little 190-yard 6-iron slice up the road, around the trees (Figure 4-15) and onto the edge of the green.

He then two-putted from the fringe of the green (Figure 4-16) for his par 5, completing one of the greatest Houdini acts I can imagine. It kept him in contention in the tournament (as I mentioned, he eventually finished in second place).

Figure 4-16: Mickelson's third shot found its way to the edge of the 13th green.

Now think about it: Without a clear and concise image of how that slice would fly (its height and when and how much it would curve) in his mind's eye before he hit it, there is no way Phil could have pulled that shot off. I'm not showing you this to make you think "Wow, this guy is amazing." No. Instead, I want you to think "Wow, being able to curve shots on demand can be a big asset. We all need to fade or draw shots from time to time in the game, so I guess I'd better learn how."

If I didn't know Phil the way I do, I might have said "no way" when "Bones" first told me about this shot, and how the ball rolled all the way down the hill. But I've seen Phil practice his slice shots. He knows how the slice and hook rules work. And they're not that difficult to learn if you spend a little time practicing them. So my comment to you is: "If he can do it, why can't you?"

Conditioning Program

FIRST WORK ON YOUR SLICE

It's now time to take this book and your 7-, 8- and 9-irons to your backyard and teach yourself how to slice and hook shots on demand. You will need a 4' by 4' by ¾" thick wood platform covered with a SYNLawn synthetic grass Fairway Mat to hit off (www.synlawngolf.com), and a dozen almostGOLF practice balls (Figure 4-17).

Figure 4-17: Eddie with clubs and almostGOLF practice balls on our SYNLawn Fairway Mat platform.

Your task is to find ample space in your yard for your grass platform, from which you can hit 20- and 30-yard shots to a target flagstick (a stick, broom, laundry basket, etc.). Then you'll need two more markers (pylons, baskets, chairs, etc.) to be visible when you set them either left or right of your target, and something tall to use as a fake tree (you can also use a real tree, if you have one) to curve your shots around (shown in Figure 4-18). You're now ready to slice and hook away.

Figure 4-18: I'm hitting draw shots around a fake tree to the flagstick on my SYNLawn green.

To work on your slice, set the outside pylon marker four steps to the left of your target laundry basket, and the second marker halfway between that and the target (the flag is in line with the obstacle tree), as seen from your Fairway Mat grass hitting platform.

Now remember the slice rule:

1. Address your almostGOLF ball and align your body and swing at the outside left pylon (Figure 4-19, yellow tape line).

Figure 4-19: Practicing an intentional slice is fun.

2. Lighten your left-hand grip and rotate your clubface open to aim at the halfway pylon (white tape line).
3. Make sure your grip is in its normal position (as when you normally hit straight shots) while maintaining the open clubface.
4. Make your normal three-quarter 8-iron swing toward the outside pylon (yellow tape line).
5. Repeat until you can slice an almostGOLF ball around the obstacle (tree) every time.

Please be aware: When you aim your body and swing at the far left pylon, and aim your clubface at the halfway pylon, your ball will start directly at the halfway pylon and begin curving toward the tree. On the golf course, remember to leave yourself plenty of room between your shot's starting line and the tree. Limbs and leaves can affect shots, and sometimes golfers focus only on missing the tree's trunk without fully accounting for the branches.

The last thing you want to do is to hit the very obstacle you're trying to miss, which is how most golfers actually mess up this shot. So give yourself room to spare until you know for sure how much and how quickly your ball will head right and slice off of your club-face.

Your slice assignment is to hit slices of all shapes and sizes—at least five hundred shots (say fifty each session)—until you feel comfortable with how far left you need to swing to produce big slices, little slices, and all of the variations in between. And you must hit at least a hundred consecutive slices without hitting the obstacle in front of you. Once you do this and feel good about your slice swing with almostGOLF balls, it's time to move on and start working on your hook.

NEXT, HIT HOOKS

Reverse the location of your alignment pylons to the other side of the tree, and hit hooks to your laundry basket target. For players whose bad shots are pull-hooks on the golf course, the feel of intentionally launching their ball to the left of their swing line, and then having it hook farther to the left, is an uncomfortable experience (I'm raising my hand, because this is me). But don't worry, you'll get used to it (Figure 4-20).

Your hook drill is the same as the slice drill—at least five hundred shots around an obstacle. As you execute these drills, try mov-

Figure 4-20: Hitting an intentional pull/hook can be mentally challenging.

ing your alignment pylons farther away from your target, for both slices and hooks. This means you will have a more severely open or closed clubface at impact, and the balls will not only start farther off your swing line, but will also have a more curving flight trajectory. Experiment and see just how far you can hook and slice your shots, because it's fun. But spend most of your practice time hitting soft fades and draws, as they are the shots you will need most often on the golf course.

While practicing with the almostGOLF balls, understand that they are significantly easier to curve than real balls. After you've gone from the extremes of hitting very small fades and draws to hitting very large slices and hooks with them, it's time to head to a real practice range and perform the same drills with real golf balls.

TAKE IT TO THE RANGE

Your first assignment at the golf course is to hit a full bucket of balls (approximately sixty) on the practice range on three different days. I know this sounds like a lot of shots to hit, but I'm telling you . . . it will be worth it. It will take less than three hours of your time, and once you do it, you'll have the ability to curve shots on demand for the rest of your golfing career.

You don't need to use alignment pylons out on the range because you can choose targets in the distance, just like you'll be doing when you're on the course. Your drill is to:

1. Choose a target—the approximate location you want your ball to finish.
2. Select a halfway target (tree, pole, bush, house) to use for your clubface alignment—the direction you want to start your shots on.
3. Double that angle and find a target tree in the distance for your body aim and swing direction.

HIT YOUR SHOTS, LEARN YOUR LESSONS

Pick your three lines (setup, halfway, and target) carefully, and start intentionally curving your shots to targets. Don't use your driver during these sessions; your sole purpose on the range is to launch fades, draws, slices, and hooks that end up landing near your intended targets with your irons. You will quickly learn how much harder it is to curve a real ball's flight trajectory than it is with the almostGOLF balls you've been using at home. You'll also discover that lower-lofted irons and utility woods are easier to curve than higher-lofted short irons and wedges. And that the harder you hit a ball, the more you can curve it (short shots like pitches and chips do not get hit very hard, and cannot be curved much).

Don't be embarrassed to stand on the practice tee and hit big hooks and slices. Players with very low handicaps do this from time to time, and you should, too. There is an additional benefit to all of this practice: It will help you understand how to hit shots straighter in the future. As you practice small draws and fades, you will notice that between those two curved trajectories is a straight shot— the one you can hit only if your clubface is exactly square to your swing path direction at impact.

You need three established directions before hitting curved-trajectory shots: one for your body aim and swing-path direction; another halfway between that and your final shot target (for aiming your clubface); and, of course, the direction of the target (or final destination of the shot).

TAKE IT TO THE COURSE

Once you've experienced hitting about two hundred successfully curved shots on the practice range, your confidence will build as your fear of this shot recedes. Then you'll be ready to tackle the course and challenge yourself to execute real shots around real trees, with your score on the line. Expect to mess up a few of these shots as you learn to incorporate this new skill into your game, but the confidence will be there for you in the long run, because you've paid your dues. You've learned why and how the shot works, and you've got the feel of doing it in your brain and body: you can play this shot.

You *know* you can now intentionally curve shots around trees, so start doing it with confidence . . . on the golf course!

CHAPTER 5

Most Feared Shot #6: Buried Lies in Sand

The Shot

WHEN AN APPROACH SHOT MISSES the green but comes in high and hard on a near vertical angle of descent, the ball will often bury or plug down in the sand (Figure 5-1). If it happens to be very soft, sugar-fine sand, this type of shot can wind up completely buried or covered over with sand. On some occasions, it can even be difficult to find.

Luckily, balls don't frequently bury in the sand. In fact, less than one in thirty sand shots are from buried lies. Still, our survey results indicate that buried lies in sand weigh heavily on the minds of many golfers: it is the sixth most feared shot in golf.

OPPOSITE: Figure 5-1: A buried lie in the sand.

Figure 5-2: When faced with a buried lie, golfers are afraid the ball may go anywhere—or nowhere at all!

Golfers don't like to play this shot (Figure 5-2) and often turn and look the other way with a big sigh and an "Oh boy, here comes disaster" when they're faced with it. This is because in the few times they've encountered the shot, they've had difficulty even getting the ball out of the sand, let alone getting it up and onto the green near the hole.

The Problem

Nearly every time they've come across the shot, the results haven't been good. Explanations range from "I bounced right over the ball and left it where it was" to "I hit right down on top of it and drove it deeper into the sand." Golfers who fear this shot don't know where to stand, where to play the ball in their stance, or how far to hit behind the ball. They're not even sure if they should hit the ball or the sand first! If it does come out, they're not sure where it will go or when it will stop.

Herein lies the problem: Most golfers don't have a clue about *how* to play this shot. They've never taken a lesson on buried lies, and they've only tried the shot a few times on their own, with little or no success.

The Solution

Not to worry! The shot isn't all that difficult, if you view success as getting the ball out of the sand and up onto the green—anywhere on the green. If you insist on getting the shot close enough to the hole to ensure a one-putt, however, then you have a much more difficult challenge.

Let me put this another way: Escaping from a buried lie is easy once you learn the proper technique, whereas getting the ball out *and* controlling precisely where it goes thereafter is something even the pros have difficulty doing.

What's the proper technique? There are three of them, actually:

1. The "splash/pop," using a heel-in-first *open* clubface.
2. The "flip," using a toe-in-first *closed* clubface.
3. The square-faced "blast."

Each of these three techniques is unique because they require different swing executions and produce different shot reactions. I'll deal with each separately in the order of how much energy and how softly each technique launches the ball from the sand. Let's begin with the softest approach first—the buried-lie escape shot most likely to stop after rolling the shortest distance.

1) THE OPEN-FACED (HEEL-IN-FIRST) "SPLASH/POP" SHOT

Most TOUR professionals play shots from buried lies with an open clubface, trying to splash the ball softly out of the sand and onto the green. Because they play on greens that are lightning fast and often miss their approach shots to the "short" side of the green (relatively close to the flagstick), they need to create an escape shot trajectory that is as high and soft as possible so the ball will stop quickly. The sand type that helps this technique is firm, yet light enough to allow the clubhead to get under the ball.

To splash a ball from a buried lie, you will want to position your ball in the middle of your stance, open the clubface so the heel of your wedge leads the club into the sand, and then "splash" your clubhead down just behind the ball as shown in Figure 5-3. The splash technique requires that the heel of the wedge enters *and* leaves the sand first. This means the clubface remains open as it splashes down into and then moves through the sand. It's still open when it exits the sand.

Figure 5-3: The heel of the club enters and leaves the sand first, in the splash shot from a buried lie.

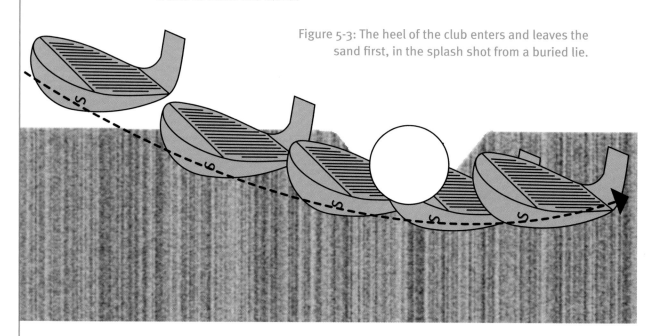

Figure 5-4: Address position for the splash shot with heel leading the clubhead (clubface open).

In the splash technique, it's imperative that the heel of the club be held ahead (in front of) the clubface at address (Figure 5-4), and then leads the open clubface throughout the entire down- and through-swing as it travels through the sand. There is only a short follow-through motion out of the sand after the splash.

THE "POP" SHOT

The "pop" shot (perfected to my knowledge by Paul Azinger) is an extreme variation of the splash shot that also requires the "heel-in-first" swing technique. The pop shot produces the softest and quickest possible stopping action from a buried lie, and will be addressed later in this section.

2) THE CLOSED-FACE, TOE-IN-FIRST "FLIP" SHOT

When a slightly longer roll-out is available (or necessary) to stop the ball close to the flagstick, TOUR professionals will sometimes use the "flip" technique for their buried sand shots. The flip technique requires that the toe of the wedge enter the sand first to cut quickly and efficiently (with low resistance) down into the sand (Figure 5-5). As the club digs down to a level just below the ball, it encounters enough resistance from the sand to rotate into a square, then open, position as it passes through where the ball was originally buried. (Note: In this flip motion, the rotating clubface never actually contacts the ball. As the face flips and passes under the ball, there is always sand between the clubface and the ball.)

Figure 5-5: In the flip shot, the toe enters the sand first and then rotates (flips) from square to open and leaves the sand last.

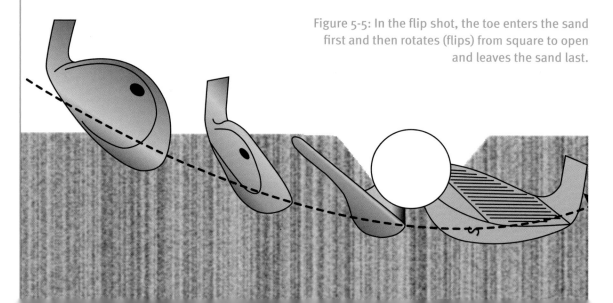

The reason the flip technique produces more carry and a longer run-out for shots (as compared to the splash technique) is because the toe of the club encounters very little resistance as it initially enters the sand. This allows the clubhead to retain more speed through the sand, and thus arrive at (and slide under) the ball with greater speed and energy. The toe-in-first flip address position is shown in Figure 5-6.

Figure 5-6: Address position for the toe-in-first flip technique.

3) THE SQUARE-FACED DIG-AND-PUSH "BLAST" SHOT

By far the most frequently used swing for extricating balls from buried lies is the square-faced "blast" technique. Most amateurs use this technique without considering (or knowing of) any other option. Pros use this technique when they want the ball to roll out on the green to distant hole locations.

When using the square-faced blast technique, a golfer should keep the following in mind:

1. The square face will encounter maximum resistance from the sand.
2. Maximum swing speed and effort will be required to dig the clubhead into and through the sand.
3. A maximum amount of sand will be trapped between the clubface and ball.
4. The ball will be launched (blasted away) from the sand on a low trajectory.
5. The ball will come out with minimum backspin.

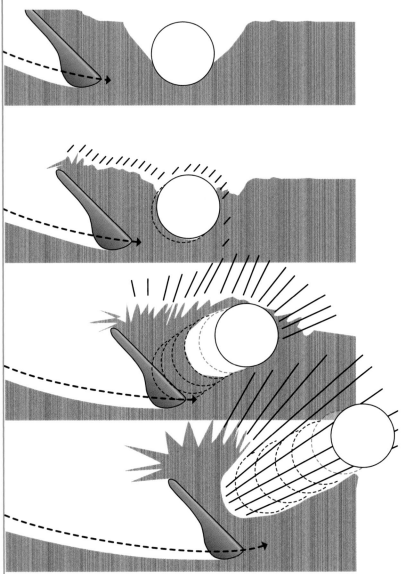

When a wedge enters the sand with its clubface square (perpendicular) to the swing motion (Figure 5-7), it encounters maximum sand resistance because its entire surface area is pushing squarely against the sand. This means that a square-faced blast swing will slow much more quickly than a splash or flip swing after the clubhead enters the sand. The clubhead must also move two to three times more sand as it passes through and gouges out its sand divot.

Figure 5-7: A square clubface encounters much more resistance from the sand than do an open or closed face.

While these differences may sound like negatives to you, they can be strong assets when the shot demands a longer roll-out on the green. This swing technique is by far the easiest way to get your sand shots to roll 60 feet across a very long green, or up a slope on a terraced green to a back pin position. The setup and address position for the square-faced dig-and-push blast shot is shown in Figure 5-8.

Figure 5-8: Address position for the square-faced blast technique.

Now that you understand what actually happens to a club as it passes through the sand during these three different shot techniques, you need to see—and internalize—what the swings will look like in motion. It's important that you study the photographs closely enough to internalize where the ball should be positioned in your stance, what the clubface should look like from your Golfer's-Eye View, where your body and swing alignment should be relative to the target, and how big a backswing and follow-through you will use for each technique.

The four things you should pay attention to when learning each shot are: 1) ball position, 2) clubface angle, 3) setup alignment, and 4) swing length. Once you understand the proper technique for playing each shot and have experienced each a few times, escaping from buried lies in the sand will become relatively routine.

How It Should Look

1) THE HEEL-IN-FIRST POP SHOT

I want to start by showing you how former PGA champion and Ryder Cup captain Paul Azinger executes his pop shot. I actually think of this as "his" pop shot, because he told me about it, then showed me how he could execute the shot out of a buried lie higher—and softer—than anyone else in the world.

When Zinger walked up to this buried lie (Figure 5-9) at East Lake Golf Club in Atlanta, he told me I wouldn't believe it, but that if he used his pop-shot technique he would have a hard time getting his ball to roll all the way to the pin on this super-fast green. He said the ball would come out so softly that it would probably stop short of the hole almost every time. (I didn't believe him at the time.)

As I watched him set up to the ball with a wide-open club-face, I said, "I know that shot—you're just going to splash it out like everybody else." I thought for sure the ball would roll well past the flagstick.

Figure 5-9: Paul Azinger faces a buried lie with a steep bank in front of him and water behind the green.

He said, "Look again, my friend. My stance is aligned more to the left (of the target) and my clubface is more open than anyone else's. I also lean forward more and follow through less than anyone else, except maybe Gary Player. And this ball will absolutely come out softer, and stop quicker, than anybody else's."

Now, most PGA TOUR players would splash this shot out with an open clubface, but Zinger was right. He leaned forward (Figure 5-10) and came into the ball on a steeper angle of attack than anyone else I'd ever seen.

Figure 5-10: Zinger sets up to pop the ball out from a buried lie, with the heel of the club entering the sand first.

Look at how open his clubface is at address from the Golfer's-Eye View (Figure 5-11). Rotate your book 45 degrees clockwise, tilt your head left, and look up at the left-hand page to see the shot he is set up to hit. Try to imagine that it's you in this bunker and that you're confident you'll get the ball out, but worried it will come out so softly that it might not get to the hole.

Figure 5-11: Golfer's-Eye View of Paul Azinger's pop shot.

Now look at his shot action from behind. He slaps his wedge down into the sand to make a big splash, and stops his swing immediately thereafter. This is important for you to pay attention to, because his pop swing has almost no follow-through on it at all (Figure 5-12). As I watched, his ball popped almost straight up and seemed to float out onto the green. It dropped down so softly, I couldn't believe it. And wouldn't you know, it rolled only three feet forward and stopped a foot short of the hole.

I have to tell you, I made Zinger do it five more times to prove his mastery of this shot to my thick brain, and he did! There was no luck involved. He owns this shot—and it works!

Figure 5-12: Nobody hits the pop shot better than Paul Azinger.

Zinger says the more he follows through, the more the ball rolls after it lands on the green (Figure 5-13). This is why, when he stops his swing immediately after impact, the ball simply pops up onto the green so softly. That's why he calls it his pop (and not splash) shot.

Figure 5-13: Zinger's pop swing motion from a face-on angle.

Figure 5-14: Tom Sieckmann's setup for a heel-in-first splash shot.

The splash shot that most PGA TOUR professionals use is very similar to the pop shot, with three minor tweaks: 1) the lean forward is still there but is slightly less pronounced; 2) the clubface angle is open but not quite as much; and 3) the follow-through is still short, but not quite as short as stopping immediately after impact.

Look at how PGA TOUR pro Tom Sieckmann sets up to splash a shot softly out of sand in Figure 5-14. In this shot, Tom had plenty of green to work with and no real danger behind the hole, so he wanted to carry the ball a little farther than Zinger did earlier. Notice how he's still leaning slightly forward and his clubface is open, just not as much as in Zinger's pop shot.

Now look from behind as we see Sieckmann splashing his buried ball out of the sand (Figure 5-15). Remember: In the splash technique, the heel of the wedge leads all the way through the sand, with the intention of producing a soft shot that won't run too far after it lands.

Figure 5-15: Sieckmann splashes the ball out from a buried lie in the sand.

Figure 5-16: Tom's splash shot lands softly, with very little roll-out.

Tom stops his follow-through shortly after his club clears the sand (Figure 5-16). Again, this splash technique brings the ball out softly with a minimum amount of forward momentum. Even though it's virtually impossible to put a significant amount of backspin on shots from buried lies, if you can bring them out softly enough, they won't roll too far.

Figure 5-17: The heel-in-first splash divot.

Please look carefully at the close-up of Sieckmann's splash divot in the sand. While the divot is approximately two inches deep (Figure 5-17), it has only splashed a minimum amount of sand out from around the clubhead's actual heel-in-first path.

It would be good for you to now compare Tom's splash swing (Figure 5-18) with that of Paul Azinger's pop swing (Figure 5-13) from earlier. When you work on your own buried-lie swings, you may want to try both of these swing actions. As a point of interest, however, the splash swing is much more useful over a larger range of golf shots, and has a greater margin for error than the pop shot.

Figure 5-18: Tom Sieckmann's heel-in-first splash shot.

Figure 5-19: Tom's setup for the toe-in-first flip shot.

For a totally opposite approach to extricating the ball from a buried lie, let's now look at the flip shot. In the flip shot, the toe of the club cuts into the sand and encounters minimum resistance until it gets fairly deep in the sand and to the ball. At that point the resistance of the sand rotates the club around into a square and then an open position (with the heel leading), as it flips the ball up and out of the sand.

Tom Sieckmann demonstrates this technique (Figure 5-19). Unlike the previous situation, where he splashed the ball out, he's got a little more room for the ball to release and roll to the flagstick, and he can carry it farther to the hole.

Tom addresses the ball with the clubface closed so that the toe of the wedge points into the sand (Figure 5-20). This is in anticipation of the toe entering and cutting deeply into the sand before the clubhead reaches the position of the ball. Tom's upper body leans slightly forward and the ball is a little back in his stance.

Figure 5-20: Tom's closed-face, toe-in position at address.

From the Golfer's-Eye View (Figure 5-21), try to imagine yourself in this position. Look down at your setup, then up to the target, then down at the ball again and imagine that you're ready to waggle and hit the shot. For future reference, the deeper the ball is buried in the sand, the more you'll want to point the toe of the club down toward the sand. This is so the toe's edge will dig more deeply before it meets serious resistance from the sand, and begins to square up and flip the ball out.

Figure 5-21: A Golfer's-Eye View of the toe-in-first flip shot.

Next, look at the view of Tom from behind as his toe-in-first swing flips the ball up and out of his buried lie (Figure 5-22).

Figure 5-22:
The flip shot
escape from a
buried lie for
Tom Sieckmann.

You'll notice that just as with the splash shot, not too much sand is spread (or blown) around his bunker divot. The club's toe cuts into the sand and scoops the ball out, carving a divot with minimal surrounding splash (Figure 5-23).

Figure 5-23 and detail: Tom's flip technique produces more roll, with minimum sand splashed from the divot.

Another point of interest for future reference: If Tom wanted to carry this shot a few feet farther, or have the ball release a few more feet after landing, all he'd have to do is make his follow-through longer. By simply making the same swing with a longer and more forceful follow-through, he would achieve more distance on the shot roll-out.

As you can see in the face-on view of his swing, the flip shot does not require a very large or violent swing (Figure 5-24). Because the toe of the wedge cuts into the sand so efficiently, it minimizes the brute force required to get the clubhead to the ball.

Figure 5-24: Tom Sieckmann's toe-in-first flip swing.

3) THE SQUARE-FACED DIG-AND-PUSH BLAST SHOT

The square-faced blast is the most used shot for playing from buried lies in sand. It's the only technique that most amateurs ever think to try, and the pros use it when they don't want the ball to stop quickly after it lands on the green. If you refer back to the illustration (Figure 5-7) at the beginning of this section, you'll notice that when the leading edge of a square-faced wedge enters the sand, it encounters maximum sand resistance to its motion. Therefore, one must always swing longer and harder (faster) when using this technique.

In Figure 5-25, you'll see a down-the-line view of Sieck's setup for a square-faced blast shot, which will fly about seven yards onto the green and then roll another 30 feet to the hole.

Figure 5-25: Setup for a square-faced blast shot from a buried lie.

From the Golfer's-Eye View, you can see that the clubface is square at address and (as you rotate this book and look up to see the target) there is room for this shot to roll to the flagstick (Figure 5-26).

Figure 5-26: Golfer's-Eye View of a square-faced blast shot.

From a face-on view, take a look at how the square-faced blast swing (Figure 5-27) compares to the less violent splash and flip swings seen earlier. See how the ball comes out hotter? While the blast technique is a simple and reliable way to get the ball out from a buried lie, don't expect the ball to stop quickly on the green after it lands.

Figure 5-27: The blast swing technique.

An Additional Shot

THE COCK-AND-POP SHOT

There is an alternative way (technique) to get out of buried lies, to the main three techniques detailed above. It's called the "cock-and-pop" shot, a compromise between the square-faced blast shot and the pop shot. The cock-and-pop utilizes a rapid and complete wrist

Figure 5-28: Address position for the cock-and-pop shot.

cock with a very short backswing, followed by a hand- and wrist-powered downswing that transmits a fair amount of force into the back of the ball. It's something you can try after you've learned the main three ways to escape from buried sand lies.

The setup for a cock-and-pop shot requires a square or slightly closed clubface, with the ball positioned well back in the stance (Figure 5-28). The concept of the shot is to make a steeply descending blow as close to the back of the ball as you dare with a high-lofted wedge (Figure 5-29). There is no follow-through. The intent is to simply squeeze the ball up and out of the sand without hitting it too far. There will be no back-spin on the ball, so if you pop it into the fringe or light rough just short of the green, it should dribble onto the green and roll a reasonable distance (at least 10 feet).

Figure 5-29: The cock-and-pop technique requires maximum wrist cock and a minimal backswing.

The advantage of the cock-and-pop method is that there's not much motion to the swing, and therefore not much that can go wrong with it. The disadvantage of this technique is that you can't carry the ball very far in the air (not much swing power), and if you enter the sand a little too far behind the ball, you may not carry it out of the bunker (Figure 5-30) at all.

Figure 5-30: The danger of the cock-and-pop technique is leaving the ball in the sand.

Conditioning Program

Once you intellectually understand the mechanics of how to get a ball out of a buried lie, and your mind's eye has a clear vision of what you should look like doing it, all that remains to conquering your fear of the shot is to ingrain the feeling of making these sand swings in your body.

This sounds simple—and it is—but it will take time and practice, plus a good dose of patience. You'll have to gather together several pieces of equipment to use in your backyard, and you'll need a significant number of practice sessions before you take your buried lie escape swing to the golf course.

First, you've got to determine which shot (splash, flip, or blast) you feel most comfortable with. This choice may depend on the particulars of each different buried lie. You'll have to try them all to see which works best for you and your golf swing. Before you do this, however, you need to establish some reasonable expectations for this shot.

By reasonable I mean that you should not expect to perform as well as the pros do, unless you practice like them. And while buried lies are not impossible to get out of, they're difficult to hit consistently close to the hole. To demonstrate this point, I jumped into a bunker and hit ten normal sand shots from perfect lies. I then hit another ten shots from buried lies to the same flagstick (I practiced both shots a few times before this exercise). I then averaged the distance from the hole for my best five shots from each lie, and marked that distance with a ball, as shown in Figure 5-31. My best five shots from perfect lies (the ball in the background) averaged about five times closer to the hole than my best five shots from buried lies (the ball in the foreground). And my worst five averages were even farther apart.

FOLLOWING PAGE: Figure 5-31: Be realistic: Your results from buried lies will be worse than those from good lies in the sand.

I also want you to follow some generic guidelines for hitting shots from buried sand lies. You should read these guidelines now, and then reread them from time to time before practicing in your backyard.

- ► **THE BETTER YOUR LIE** (the higher the ball rests on top of the sand), the farther forward you should position the ball in your stance.
- ► **THE WORSE YOUR LIE** (the deeper your ball sits down in sand), the farther back in your stance the ball should be positioned.
- ► **THE FARTHER FORWARD** the ball is positioned in your stance, the more you should open the clubface.
- ► **THE FARTHER BACK** the ball is positioned in your stance, the more you should close the clubface, unless you're hitting the splash/pop shot.

THE MORE YOU OPEN THE CLUBFACE:
- ► The more left you must aim
- ► The shallower the club will move through the sand
- ► The higher the trajectory of the shot
- ► The more backspin the shot will have
- ► The softer the shot will land

THE MORE YOU CLOSE THE CLUBFACE:
- ► The more square or right you must aim
- ► The deeper your club will dig into the sand
- ► The lower the trajectory of the shot
- ► The farther the ball will roll after landing

THE LONGER YOUR FOLLOW-THROUGH:
- ► The less likely you are to leave your ball in the sand
- ► The longer your roll-out distance will be

THE SHORTER YOUR FOLLOW-THROUGH:
- ► The less forward momentum your shot will have
- ► The softer the shot will land
- ► The more likely you are to leave your ball in the sand

A four-inch-deep tray filled with sand (preferably the type of sand you encounter on your local golf course), measuring a minimum of twelve inches wide by thirty inches long, is required for backyard practice. You can build your own with plywood and lumber from Lowe's or Home Depot.

I have only one assignment for you to accomplish to conquer your fear of buried lies, and that's to spend 15 minutes a night at least once a week (for a full golf season) hitting almostGOLF balls from buried lies in the sand. If you don't have a platform and sand tray (and you probably don't), then you can build one (Figure 5-32). (Note: I already know you won't drive to the golf course often enough to learn these buried-lie escape techniques there).

Figure 5-32: A sand tray for backyard practice with almostGOLF balls.

I want to leave you with one thought for future sand play. Please become familiar with all of the techniques discussed above (even though one will probably become your favorite) (Figure 5-33), because you never know which one you'll need on the golf course.

Figure 5-33: There are good options available when confronted with a buried lie; please learn them all.

Actually, I think you'll find it fun to splash, flip, and blast your fear of buried lies away. Of course, the more sand shots you hit in your backyard, the sooner you can be proud of your sand game on the course. And finally, a bit of encouragement, because I know most amateurs dread the sand, not to mention the buried lie in the sand: If you persevere, build a backyard sand tray, and perform the drills as I've suggested, you'll never have to worry about buried lies again!

CHAPTER 6

5

Most Feared Shot #5: The
High, Soft, Cut-Lob Shot

ATTEMPTING A VERY HIGH, SOFT LOB SHOT that stops quickly on the green strikes fear in the hearts of many golfers. But before we detail the shot itself, I want to make sure you're clear on what this shot is. I can loft a high, soft shot with my 64-degree X-Wedge using my normal wedge swing and keeping the clubface square. But that's not the shot golfers fear. Nor is it a flop shot.

The shot our survey golfers fear most is one that requires them to lay open their clubface and cut across the ball, producing a higher trajectory shot than their normal swing can generate. They fear hitting cut-lob shots. And for the record: When someone hits a shot that flies even higher than the extra-high cut-lob, we refer to it as a "Mickelson Flop" (Figure 6-1).

Figure 6-1: Phil Mickelson demonstrates the "Mickelson Flop" directly over my head on a Golf Channel show.

Figure 6-2: Lofting a cut-lob shot over one bunker and short of another.

To be clear about the shot I'm talking about, look at the cut-lob I'm hitting in Figure 6-2 over one greenside bunker and short of another. This green limits me to about a 10-foot area where I can land and stop my ball, if it's going to end up anywhere near the flagstick.

Figure 6-3: The high, soft cut-lob shot down to a hole in a severe swale.

In Figure 6-3, I'm preparing to loft a cut-lob shot to the upslope behind the pin, so I can draw the ball back toward the hole. It's my best chance to get it close: If I land my ball on the downslope short of the pin, it will roll too far past the flagstick.

The Problem

The cut-lob shot is one of the frequently needed—but seldom-used—shots in golf. Why does this shot strike fear into golfers the world over? Because, similar to a greenside sand shot, there is enough force in the cut-lob swing that if club-to-ball contact is not good, it can send the ball either 50 yards over the green or leave it three feet in front of you. The misses are dramatic with this shot—and therefore embarrassing. A situation that illustrates the need for the cut-lob is shown in Figure 6-4. When I first pitched a normal wedge shot onto this firm, sloping green, my ball rolled 20 feet past the hole.

Figure 6-4: The severe downslope kicks my standard pitch shot 20 feet past the hole.

The best way for me to get up and down from the rough would've been to play a very high cut-lob shot with an L-wedge. With a soft, extra-high trajectory, I could land my ball on the upslope behind the hole and bring it back to the flagstick.

Most golfers would never try a cut-lob here for fear of skulling (hitting the top half of the ball) or fatting (taking turf behind) the shot. The root of their struggles (and subsequent fear) comes from a belief that to hit a higher-than-normal-trajectory shot, one needs to play the ball forward in one's stance.

MOVING THE BALL FORWARD TO HIT IT HIGHER IS WRONG!

You've probably heard or read somewhere that "to hit a high shot, you should move the ball forward in your stance." So the first time you tried to hit a shot high, you positioned the ball up in your stance, and naturally hit behind it. Then on your next few attempts you lunged forward to avoid hitting behind the ball, then cupped your wrists to help get the ball up into the air.

By incorporating a lunge and cup into your swing technique, you make the high, soft shot extremely difficult to execute. You subsequently hit a lot of fat and skulled shots, which creates an expectation of bad results and fear. It's a vicious chain reaction of errors, all caused by the mistaken assumption that you need to play the ball forward in your stance in order to produce a high-trajectory shot (Figure 6-5).

In an attempt to hit high, soft pitch shots, golfers will mistakenly:

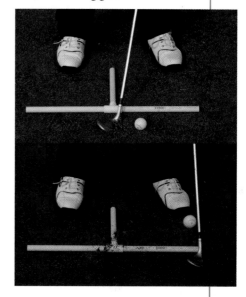

Figure 6-5: When the ball is forward in your stance, it's very easy to hit behind it.

1. Move the ball forward in their stance.
2. Address the ball with a square clubface.
3. Aim directly at the target.
4. Lunge forward on their downswing to avoid hitting behind the ball.
5. Cup their left wrist through impact to help the ball fly higher.
6. Hit fat behind the ball and "fat-chunk" it, or . . .
7. Skull it over the green.

This misconception about ball position is so prevalent that you need to understand why it's wrong, and why it produces such disastrous results.

A NORMAL SWING ARC BOTTOMS OUT
JUST FORWARD OF STANCE CENTER

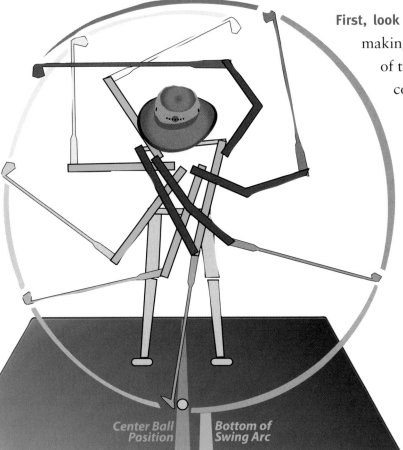

Center Ball Position

Bottom of Swing Arc

First, look at the stick figure in Figure 6-6 making a full wedge swing. The path of the clubhead does not trace out a completely perfect circle, because cocking the wrists on the backswing flattens the top out into something of an ellipse.

The importance of this figure, however, is to illustrate that when the golfer's wrists uncock near the swing bottom before impact, the arc of the clubhead's path *really does* become a circle. And it bottoms out about four inches past impact. You can see this in a close-up at the bottom of the figure. Thus, in a normal swing with the ball positioned precisely in the center of the stance (ball #1), the clubhead will contact the ball on a slightly descending angle and hit it solidly.

But, take the same perfect swing at ball #2 positioned farther forward in the golfer's stance, and it produces either a fat or a skulled shot.

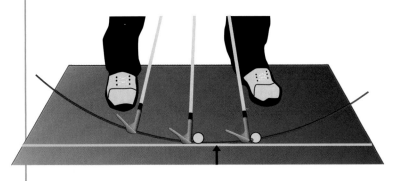

Figure 6-6: A normal swing contacts ball #1 solidly, but hits ball #2 fat because it's positioned too far forward in the stance.

CUPPING (BREAKING DOWN) THE LEAD WRIST MAKES THINGS WORSE

Now imagine what happens if the golfer's left (lead) wrist breaks down prematurely in an attempt to add loft to the shot. This causes the clubhead to bottom out even earlier in the swing (farther behind the ball), again leading to fat contact. The farther forward you position the ball in your stance, the easier it is to hit the turf behind the ball, and the more difficult it is to make solid contact.

The Solution

Thankfully, there is a better way to hit shots higher when the normal loft on your club won't suffice. And it's easy, too.

AIM LEFT AND OPEN YOUR CLUBFACE

To hit higher than normal shots: 1) aim left; 2) position the ball precisely in the center of your stance, between your ankles; 3) open your clubface so it points to your target, and 4) swing away. The higher you want to hit the shot, the farther you aim left and the more you open the clubface. I know this sounds simple, and it is. Here's why.

If you look at the overhead view down on three golfers' hats (Figure 6-7, next page), you'll notice that all three golf swings have the same swing arc (red). The only differences between the golfers are the face-angles of the club, the direction of the golfer's swing arcs are aimed (yellow), and the directions the balls fly away in.

Figure 6-7: The best way to hit a cut-lob shot is to aim left and open the clubface.

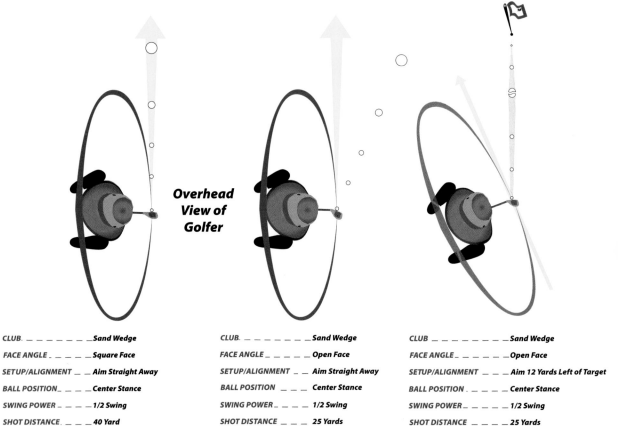

Overhead
View of
Golfer

CLUB. _ _ _ _ _ _ _Sand Wedge
FACE ANGLE . _ _ _ _Square Face
SETUP/ALIGNMENT _ _ Aim Straight Away
BALL POSITION_ _ _ _Center Stance
SWING POWER _ _ _ _1/2 Swing
SHOT DISTANCE. _ _ _40 Yard
SHOT DIRECTION _ _ _ Ball Flies Straight to Target

CLUB. _ _ _ _ _ _ _Sand Wedge
FACE ANGLE _ _ _ _ _Open Face
SETUP/ALIGNMENT _ _ Aim Straight Away
BALL POSITION _ _ _ _Center Stance
SWING POWER_ _ _ _ 1/2 Swing
SHOT DISTANCE _ _ _ 25 Yards
SHOT DIRECTION _ _ _ Ball Flies 12 Yards Right
                    of Target

CLUB _ _ _ _ _ _ _ _Sand Wedge
FACE ANGLE_ _ _ _ _Open Face
SETUP/ALIGNMENT _ _ _Aim 12 Yards Left of Target
BALL POSITION . _ _ _ _Center Stance
SWING POWER_ _ _ _ _ 1/2 Swing
SHOT DISTANCE _ _ _ _25 Yards
SHOT DIRECTION _ _ _Ball Flies Straight Away
                    to Target

STRAIGHT AIM: BALL CENTERED, CLUBFACE SQUARE

Look at the image on the left of Figure 6-7 and assume our golfer is swinging a sand wedge, is aimed straight away, and is playing the ball centered in his stance. His clubface is square to the target as he makes a nice half-swing and hits a beautiful 40-yard shot straight forward. This is how this golfer hits a simple normal, straight-forward pitch shot.

STRAIGHT AIM: BALL CENTERED, CLUBFACE OPEN

Next, look at our center golfer in Figure 6-7 making an identical swing with the same alignment and ball position as the golfer on the left, except with an open clubface (aimed right of his swing direction). Because the face is open, the ball will fly higher than normal and to the right, and travel only 25 yards (instead of 40). His ball flew higher and to the right because the face of his sand wedge was wide open, which creates more loft than normal and was aimed right at impact.

LEFT AIM: BALL CENTERED; CLUBFACE OPEN

Finally, take a look at the third golfer's swing on the right of Figure 6-7. Again, our golfer makes the same half-wedge swing, but this time both his stance and swing direction (yellow) are aimed left of the target. The ball remains in the center of his stance (so his normal swing will hit it solidly) and the face is open. In this instance, the shot will fly higher than normal and carry 25 yards directly at the flagstick. He has just executed a high, soft 25-yard cut-lob shot the easy way.

DON'T CHANGE YOUR SWING

To hit a cut-lob shot, you don't have to make a different swing motion that "cuts across" your normal setup and body alignment. And there's no need to lunge at the ball or cup your wrists. You simply aim and swing to the left of your target with a normal swing and an open clubface. The clubhead will cut across your intended target line, and since the face is open, the shot will launch higher than normal while flying straight to the target.

There's one more thing you should understand before I show you how the cut-lob shot looks when executed by some of the game's best players. I want you to know why so many golfers mistakenly think pros play the ball forward in their stances when hitting extra-high shots.

YOU CAN'T SEE BALL POSITION UNLESS YOU KNOW WHERE THE CAMERA IS

Take a look at our golfer from an overhead view in Figure 6-8, only this time notice that there's a TV camera stationed directly in front of him (face-on to his target line). In the left image, our golfer aims and swings straight at his target and hits a normal trajectory shot right down the target line. His clubface was square to his swing line, and his ball flew straight to the target.

In the right image, his target is on the same line but there is a tree in his way. So he decides to hit a cut-lob shot over the tree to his target. He aims both his body and swing to the left of his target line, checks his ball position to make sure it's perfectly centered in his stance, opens his clubface, and swings away. The ball launches high over the tree and directly to the target. The point is that the golfer played both shots from the exact same position in the grass, and both balls were centered in his stance; the only differences between the two shots were that the golfer on the right aimed and swung left with an open clubface, and he also swung harder on his cut-lob swing.

But now look at what our television camera saw looking at the two shots from its face-on position. On the left image the ball appears on TV to be centered in the golfer's stance, which it really is. On the right image the ball appears on TV to be well forward in the golfer's stance (off his left foot), which it really isn't. In fact, in the right image the ball is still centered relative to the golfer's stance and swing (red dashed line).

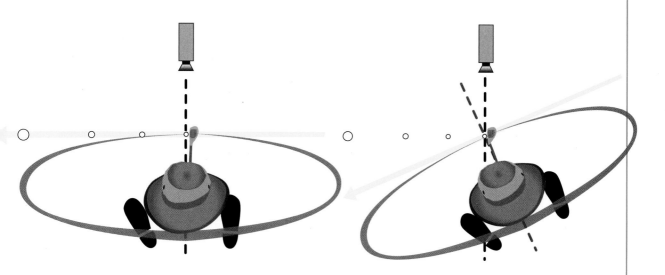

Figure 6-8: A face-on camera position makes the ball appear on TV as centered for a normal shot (left), but forward in our golfer's stance for the cut-lob shot (right).

How It Should Look

Let's go back to the earlier pitch shot I hit onto a severe downslope (see Figure 6-4, page 194). The first time I hit this shot, I set up to it assuming that my normal L-wedge setup (Figure 6-9), grip, centered ball position, and swing would get the ball close. I landed the ball on the downslope, and it bounced way forward and rolled 20 feet past the hole. I quickly realized that no matter where I landed the ball on this downslope, it would roll too far. I couldn't stop it anywhere near the hole with this approach from the rough.

Figure 6-9 and inset: My L-wedge setup, grip, and ball position for a normal pitch shot.

But then I changed my approach. I decided to aim left, open my clubface, and hit a cut-lob shot. If you compare my setup from Figure 6-9 above (standard L-wedge pitch) to Figure 6-10 (cut-lob shot), you'll see the same ball and hand positions for both shots (remember, the camera is making the ball position appear forward in Figure 6-10). In reality, only the alignment (aimed left), clubface position (open), and length of my swing (because the clubface is open the shot flies higher and shorter, so I need to make a bigger swing) are different for the cut-lob shot.

Figure 6-10 and inset: With my stance and swing aimed left, the clubface open, and my ball position centered, I'm ready to launch my cut-lob shot.

By flying a cut-lob onto the upslope past the flagstick (Figure 6-11 below and opposite), the upslope became a backstop to help bring the ball back to the hole (with the help of a small amount of backspin).

Figure 6-11: Using a cut-lob trajectory, I'm able to use the upslope as a backstop and bring the ball back to the hole.

From the Golfer's-Eye View the cut-lob setup may look strange to you, but it looks absolutely normal to me. I've been hitting cut-lob shots for a long time, and when I look down to check my alignment and ball position (right-hand page, Figure 6-12), it doesn't seem out of the ordinary. Then when I look up at the target (left-hand page, make sure to rotate book clockwise 45 degrees and tilt head left), I only have to judge how big a swing I need to make to carry the shot past the pin.

Figure 6-12: The Golfer's-Eye View of a cut-lob shot.

Viewing my swing motion from face-on (Figure 6-13), it almost looks as though I'm hitting a normal 45-yard wedge shot. What I'm really doing, however, is using my regular 45-yard wedge swing, aiming left, opening my clubface, and lofting a 25-yard cut-lob shot.

Figure 6-13: My 25-yard cut-lob shot has the look of a longer wedge swing.

A LONGER SWING GIVES YOU MORE CONTROL

One might assume that a longer swing is a drawback to this shot, but it's really not. Having the ball centered in your stance and being able to use your normal swing makes the shot as easy as any wedge shot to execute. It also gives you the confidence to swing as freely as you like, promoting better distance control on shorter shots. (When your swing gets shorter, it becomes difficult to gauge how much power to put into the shot.)

Once you discover how easy it is to hit a cut-lob, you'll begin to have fun with it. As greens keep getting faster every year, and new groove regulations make it more difficult to put spin on the ball, you're going to need this shot more and more.

Additional Shots

I've been talking to you about hitting high, soft cut-lob shots around the greens, but the exact same setup and swing principles (aim left, ball centered, clubface open) apply to creating higher trajectories with essentially any short-iron shot (Figure 6-14).

Figure 6-14: Cut-lob setup and swing with an 8-iron.

THE CUT-LOB SWING IS EASIER

The cut-lob technique eliminates all the difficulties you encounter when you adjust your swing for a forward ball position. Imagine having to lunge at the ball and cup your wrists to hit an 8-iron up and over a tree. No, thank you! You're much better off using an open-faced cut-lob swing (Figure 6-15) with a centered ball position.

Figure 6-15: With a cut-lob swing, I can carry this tree and the water with an 8-iron.

The cut-lob technique also works well when you need to play high-trajectory shots from the sand. PGA TOUR pro Tom Sieckmann is facing such a shot below (Figure 6-16) from a 22-foot-deep bunker left of the 16th green at the PGA West Stadium Course in La Quinta, California.

Figure 6-16: Six-foot-four Tom Sieckmann looks 22 feet up to the 16th green at the Stadium Course at PGA West.

From the sand, all Tom can see is the top of the flagstick. He needs to get the ball up quickly to clear the grass bank and land safely on the green (Figure 6-17).

Figure 6-17: With the flagstick barely visible, the only play here is to use a cut-lob technique from the sand.

If you ever find yourself in a similar situation, have faith in your cut-lob technique. Aim left, make sure your ball position is centered in your stance, and open your clubface—in this instance, as wide as you can, so that it almost lies flat (Figure 6-18).

Figure 6-18: With the cut-lob shot, the ball should be played in the center of your stance.

As you learned earlier, a photograph or a TV camera can make it appear as if the ball is forward in a golfer's stance. In Figure 6-18 above, it's pretty clear that the ball is centered in Tom's stance. But in the next photograph (Figure 6-19), you can see how the camera angle makes it appear as if the ball is forward, not centered.

Figure 6-19: Tom's ball appears to be forward in his stance from this camera view, but it's actually centered.

It's a beautiful thing to watch a PGA TOUR player make an intimidating shot look easy. Tom can hit cut-lob wedge shots off grass lies all day, and he also hits them nicely with the same swing from sand (Figure 6-20). Notice that his swing and stance are both aimed left, but that the shot flies straight to the target because his clubface was wide open.

Armed with his cut-lob setup, Tom is able to make his normal wedge swing to launch the ball on a nice, high trajectory up to the green (Figure 6-21).

Figure 6-20: While Sieck's swing and clubhead travel to the left, the ball flies directly at the hole.

Figure 6-21: Sieckmann's cut-lob bunker shot from a face-on view.

Now let me show you how a friend of mine executes the cut-lob. Have you ever met lefty Phil Mickelson's right-handed twin brother? Well, here he is, righty Phil Mickelson (Figure 6-22). We simply reversed the film on these three images (note the backward writing on his hat and golf bag) to show how the real Phil would look if he were right-handed.

Figure 6-22: Phil Mickelson's cut-lob swing reversed to appear right-handed.

I know I keep preaching the same three setup principles for the cut-lob shot, but they're all you really need to master high-trajectory shots with confidence. To review, you want to aim your body and swing to the left (right for left-handers), center the ball in your stance, and open your clubface. It's really that simple. The higher you want to launch your shots (Figure 6-23), the farther left you aim and the more you open the clubface. You won't see anyone hit shots higher than Phil when he launches a cut-lob.

Figure 6-23: The Mickelson cut-lob.

Phil practices this shot wherever he goes because he uses it so often in tournament play (Figures 6-24A and B). It comes in handy when you need to land the ball softly and keep the roll to a minimum on firm greens.

Figures 6-24A and 6-24B: Mickelson at the Open Championship polishing his cut-lob shots.

After the 2008 U.S. Open at Torrey Pines in San Diego, I went out for Golf Channel to duplicate the shot that lost the tournament for Rocco Mediate in his playoff with Tiger Woods. I found the spot near the bleachers (Figure 6-25) from where Rocco played a normal trajectory wedge shot that ended up 20 feet past the pin (he landed it short of the green and let it bounce up). He missed his putt for par, but had he played a cut-lob wedge from here, I think he might have been able to save his par and continue his incredible battle against Tiger.

Figure 6-25: A perfect spot for a cut-lob.

When you have confidence that you can aim left, open your clubface, and use your normal wedge swing to hit high, soft, cut-lobs, it can make treacherous-looking shots seem simple to play (Figure 6-26).

Figure 6-26: A reliable cut-lob shot can get you out of trouble (Escondido Country Club's 17th hole).

Conditioning Program

You've seen how the proper setup can make the cut-lob a relatively simple shot to execute, and you've read what not to do when you want to loft a shot high up into the air: *Don't* play the ball forward in your stance! But it's all been intellectual recognition so far, and it's often easier to intellectualize things than to actually do them. Until you learn the feel of making hundreds of cut-lob swings successfully, you're not about to replace your fear of this shot with confidence.

Here's the program I recommend to develop and groove your cut-lob swing:

Section 6-1: Steps for grooving your new cut-lob swing

IN YOUR BACKYARD:

1. Confirm your normal wedge swing and centered ball position with almostGOLF balls.
2. Learn how far to aim left by measuring your drift angle to the right with almostGOLF balls.
3. Test to find out how high you can launch your cut-lob shots over a screen with almostGOLF balls.
4. Test your aim and launch angle with almostGOLF balls, hitting to a target.
5. Confirm your aim and launch angle with real golf balls, hitting to a target.
6. Play cut-lob games with real golf balls in your backyard (only if you have the space).

AT THE GOLF COURSE:

1. Hit three buckets of cut-lob shots on the practice tee.
2. Find a tree, a hedge, or anything you can't damage and practice hitting cut-lobs over it.
3. Go out on the course in the evenings and hit realistic cut-lob shots. Hit three balls each time to different targets.

Now, let me walk you through each step, one at a time, to make sure you understand them. Remember, it will take you some time to learn the correct feel for this shot, and getting the proper feedback from your practice is crucial to future performance. Practicing with immediate, accurate, and reliable feedback is what you need to master the cut-lob swing, and it's the only way to eliminate your fear of it.

STEP #1: START BY CONFIRMING YOUR
BALL POSITION AND NORMAL WEDGE SWING

First, you need to purchase (or build) a 4 x 4-foot plywood sheet (¾-inch thick) and cover it with a SYNLawn synthetic Fairway Mat (www.synlawngolf.com). Along one edge place a strip of tape aimed precisely at your target (Figure 6-27, white strip). The mat is required to save your lawn from getting torn up with divots, and the target line makes forming proper alignment habits much easier. Next, place two more strips of tape on the mat: a yellow strip aimed along your swing line (for now, place it just inside the white target line), and a red strip running just inside your toe line at address. The yellow line indicates where your swing is aimed, and the red strip runs parallel to it to make sure that your body is also aimed properly during practice.

Figure 6-27: Backyard setup on hitting mat for cut-lob practice: white = target line; yellow = swing line; red = body (feet) line

Once you have your target (in Figure 6-27, the flagstick) and hitting mat in place and properly aligned, you're ready to start. First, hit normal wedge shots from your traditional stance and centered ball position (Figure 6-28). If you can't hit these shots well, you should work on your normal pitch shot (see Shot #8 in this book) before worrying about your cut-lob swing.

Figure 6-28: A normal pitch shot with the face square: swing line (yellow) and ball trajectory travel along the target line (white).

STEP #2: MEASURE YOUR DRIFT ANGLE

To measure how far right your shots will drift when you open the clubface, follow the six steps listed below in your backyard. This will start the process of building feel and confidence in your ability to execute a cut-lob swing.

Section 6-2: How to measure your drift angle with almostGOLF balls

1. Hit half-swing L-wedge shots straight at your target using almost-GOLF balls.
2. Make the same swings with a half-open clubface to establish your half-lob shot-drift angle (the degree to which your ball drifts to the right of your target).
3. Make the same half-swings again, this time with a wide-open clubface (laid flat, like a pancake) to establish your full-open cut-lob shot-drift angle.
4. Measure your two drift angles.
5. Reset your aim (to the left of your target) based on your drift angle.
6. Verify your half-open and wide-open cut-lob shot alignments to your target, first with almostGOLF balls, then with real balls.

Here are these six steps in further detail:

Step 1: Hit ten almostGOLF balls with a half-sand-wedge swing straight at your target flag. You hit these shots with your body and swing aimed straight at the target with a square clubface, and the ball positioned precisely in the middle of your stance. Try to fly the almostGOLF balls to the target, and make sure you're hitting them in the direction of your target flag.

Step 2: Repeat the same ten shots as above, except now lay your clubface halfway open relative to your target flag. (Make sure to do this before you take your grip.) As a result, all ten shots should fly (drift) to the right of your target (Figure 6-29), even though your stance and your swing lines are still aimed at the flag.

Figure 6-29: With a halfway-open clubface (body and swing aimed at flag), your shots will drift to the right and fly slightly shorter.

Don't worry about how much your shots drift right, just make sure you're aimed properly and swing straight at the target with the clubface halfway open to the right.

Step 3: Repeat the same ten shots as above, except now lay your clubface wide open relative to your target flag and swing. All ten shots should now drift even farther to the right of your target (Figure 6-30), despite your stance and swing being still aimed at the flag.

Figure 6-30: With a wide-open clubface, shots drift significantly to the right, even though my stance and swing direction are still straight at the target.

Step 4: Next, place markers down on the grass in the center of your shot group to signify the average drift of your two ten-shot patterns. The distance between each marker (shown as cones in Figure 6-31) and your target flag is the average drift angle of your two (halfway-open vs. wide-open) cut-lob shots.

Figure 6-31: Drift angles (halfway open clubface = solid line, wide-open clubface = dashed line) are a measure of how far right your cut-lobs fly relative to your aim and swing direction.

Each drift-angle distance is a measure of how far right of your aim and swing direction each shot flies. This is the distance you must aim and swing to the left of your target on the golf course, when you want to hit cut-lobs to a flagstick.

Step 5: Pick up your drift-angle markers and move them to the other side of your target flag. Place them the same distances left of your target as the drift-angles were to the right of the target. Now go back and realign your swing line (yellow tape) and toe line (red tape) on your hitting platform so that your feet, body and swing are precisely aimed at the farthest left marker from your target (Figure 6-32). This setup will allow you to aim and swing directly at the left-most marker (with your wedge face wide open) and have your cut-lobs fly directly at your target.

Step 6: Hit enough almostGOLF balls to develop a good feel for how far left you need to aim your half-open and wide-open cut-lob swings to fly shots to the target. Then start hitting real golf balls to the same target. Notice how they fly almost the same distance. Continue practicing this way until you feel as comfortable with real balls as you do with almostGOLF balls. You'll need to remember that the alignment you're learning (the amount left you aim and swing) is an angle, not a distance. This means the farther you are from your target, the farther left you must aim (albeit at the same angle) to hit cut-lobs to the target.

Figure 6-32: Aim left and swing left to launch cut-lobs at the target with a wide-open club face.

STEP #3: LEARN HOW HIGH YOUR CUT-LOB SHOTS LAUNCH WITH ALMOSTGOLF BALLS

Next, you need to revert to using almostGOLF balls and spend some time learning how quickly you can launch your shots up into the air. This practice and experience is vital to your future success with this shot. Although you won't always be hitting over obstacles, the more familiar you become with the flight trajectory of your shots, the better you will be able to predict their stopping behavior on a green.

When launching a cut-lob shot, remember that the more you lay the face of the club open, the higher and shorter the shot will fly, and the farther left you must aim to hit it at your target. So the more you open the clubface, the longer you'll have to make your swing in order to fly the ball all the way to your target. It's all a function of how much you lay the face open to create loft. Notice how my 64-degree X-Wedge creates a higher launch angle (i.e., more loft) when I dial the face from square to halfway open to wide open in Figure 6-33 below.

Figure 6-33: An orange floatie pointing perpendicular to my clubface shows how the club's loft changes as I open the face more and more.

As you play with the loft on your clubface, I recommend that you learn how high you can launch cut-lob shots with each clubface position. In Figure 6-34 below, I've assembled an easily adjustable height screen in my backyard by taping a sheet between two camera tripods.

Figure 6-34: Make some kind of adjustable-height obstacle in your backyard.

With my screen in place, I simply use my open-faced cut-lob swing to loft almostGOLF balls over it to my target (Figure 6-35).

Figure 6-35: I have no trouble lofting shots over a chest-high screen.

As I raise the screen over my head however (Figure 6-36A), I find I must open the clubface even more, aim farther left, and make longer swings to hit shots over the screen and to my target (Figure 6-36B).

Figure 6-36A: I've raised the screen so it's over my head.

Figure 6-36B: A seven-foot-tall screen placed about ten feet in front of me is still no problem.

If I really want to challenge my cut-lob swing action, I can raise it even higher (Figure 6-37A). I can clear the nine-foot-tall screen when it's ten feet in front of my ball, but I have to make a good swing and launch the ball almost straight up in the air to do it (Figure 6-37B).

Figure 6-37A: Nine feet is as high as I can get my screen.

Figure 6-37B: I have to launch the ball up very quickly to clear the screen at nine feet high, when it is ten feet in front of me.

At the point where you start to hit shots consistently over your makeshift high screen, you should again increase the difficulty. You need to know for sure how high is too high for your cut-lob swing (Figure 6-38). When I move my nine-foot-high screen in closer, I can make it so difficult that only the Phil Mickelsons of the world could clear it!

Figure 6-38: This screen is too high for my cut-lob shot to clear. The almostGOLF ball hit the screen and bounced back toward me.

STEP #4: TEST YOUR AIM LEFT AND LAUNCH ANGLE TOGETHER WITH ALMOSTGOLF BALLS TO A TARGET

Once you learn how far left to aim, and how high you can hit a cut-lob shot, you can start practicing and grooving your cut-lob swing. At this point, you need to spend ten sessions of at least thirty shots each hitting almostGOLF balls to a target. No skulling or hitting any shots fat. This may take some time—a week, a month, or six months—but get it done.

STEP #5: CONFIRM YOUR CUT-LOB SHOT WITH REAL GOLF BALLS, HITTING TO A TARGET

Your next step is to use real golf balls in your practice sessions, with the same requirements in place as in Step #4. Spend ten sessions of at least thirty shots each hitting real golf balls to a target, without skulling or hitting your shots fat (Figure 6-39).

Figure 6-39:
Use real golf balls in your practice sessions, hitting to targets.

STEP #6: PLAY CUT-LOB GAMES WITH REAL GOLF BALLS IN YOUR BACKYARD

You should by now be starting to gain some real confidence in your cut-lob. Try hitting shots from different lies, as in Figures 6-40 and 6-41 below. As you continue to practice in your backyard, remember these two things: 1) Always check your swing and body alignment relative to your clubface and the target; and 2) NEVER hit a shot without checking that your ball position is centered in your stance. Also, it would be good to get someone to compete with you if you can. It's more fun and helps prepare you for the pressure you will face on the golf course.

Figure 6-40: I call this my "Sweet Tee" because it's in the shade; very inviting when practicing in the heat in Austin, Texas.

Figure 6-41 inset: A cut-lob from my Sweet-Tee, as viewed from behind.

Figure 6-41: Hitting cut-lobs from my Sweet Tee to a green sloping away from me.

NOW GO TO THE GOLF COURSE

Once you feel confident enough that you can make reasonably good cut-lob swings in your backyard, you need to head to the golf course and reinforce your confidence. The first place to try it is on the practice tee.

STEP #1: HIT THREE BUCKETS OF BALLS ON THE PRACTICE TEE

Hit three full buckets (yes, three) of cut-lob shots on the practice range. Play to several different distances and don't worry about a target or anything very precise. Give yourself plenty of good lies, and several not-so-good ones. Try to get into the rhythm of launching cut-lobs consistently. This exercise will be fun if you let yourself enjoy it.

STEP #2: FIND A TREE, HEDGE, OR SOMETHING ELSE TO HIT OVER

After hitting three buckets on the range to no specific target, you need to find something to hit over (Figure 6-42). Start far away and experience success hitting over your obstacle, then move closer. (You may be surprised at how close you can be and still be able to hit shots over trees on the golf course).

Figure 6-42: Find a tall tree to hit cut-lob shots over in your practice.

STEP #3: GO OUT ON THE COURSE IN THE EVENINGS AND HIT THREE BALLS AT A TIME

You're now ready to take the final step of your conditioning program, which is to take your new cut-lob swing out onto the course and practice shots that you'll be playing in the future under real scoring conditions (Figure 6-43). You should do this in the evenings on the front nine of your home course (after the last group has teed off) or on the back nine early in the mornings (before any players reach that point on the course) so you can hit three shots at a time without bothering anyone else.

It's important that you only hit three balls to any one position on a green, and fix all of the pitch marks that your cut-lob shots make on the greens. (If you don't fix them, you don't deserve to practice on the course.)

Figure 6-43: A cut-lob shot over a bunker at PGA National in Palm Beach Gardens, Florida.

Figure 6-44: Can you be trusted to loft a cut-lob shot over my head from 4 feet away?

You're now ready to play the cut-lob shot without fear. And once you're past the fear, you never know when I might need someone to flop one over my head for the Golf Channel (Figure 6-44). Now wouldn't that be great if you had the confidence to hit the cut-lob shot that you used to fear, on TV?

I think you can do it!

CHAPTER 7

Most Feared Shot #4: Downhill Lies

4

The Shot

AS I STAND IN THE fairway and survey my approach shot to the ninth green at Hamilton Farm Golf Club (Figure 7-1), I become aware of three things: 1) the overwhelming beauty of the course; 2) the copious danger into which I can hit this shot (greenside bunkers, water, tall grass); and 3) the severe downslope my ball sits on.

Figure 7-1: A beautiful but dangerous shot at
Hamilton Farm Golf Club in Gladstone, New Jersey.

Downhillers are not my favorite shots in golf. I've had lots of bad experiences playing these shots during my career, and I can certainly understand why golfers fear them. I used to have serious knee problems, and as you will learn later, a golfer's lead (downhill) knee plays a big role in executing shots off downhill-sloping lies.

Downhill lies are difficult for all kinds of golfers, not just those with knee problems. Downslopes don't discriminate—high- and low-handicappers, left- and right-handers, tall and short golfers, and males and females have all told us they fear downhill lies. This shot category garnered enough votes in our surveys to qualify as the fourth most feared shot in golf.

The Problem

On downhill lies (Figure 7-2), the tendency for most golfers is to hit the ground behind the ball before their club actually gets to the ball. After they've done this a few times they'll do anything to avoid hitting the next one fat, so they overcompensate in their swing and hit the ball thin or top it. Once this occurs, they don't know what to do next, so they get into what my mother (who never swore) used to call a "mell of a hess."

There is a secondary problem that some golfers experience on downhill shots, and that's keeping their balance after they hit the shot. This is understandable, because at the finish of all good swings, golfers end up standing with most of their weight on their forward foot. On downhill shots, because the forward foot is lower than usual, the force of gravity not only assists them in turning into their follow-through, it also pulls them off balance in the downhill direction of the hill.

So with fat and thin shots, overcompensations, and poor balance, golfers begin to dread and then fear downhill shots.

Figure 7-2: Using my normal stance and swing on a downslope, I have a great chance to hit "fat" behind the ball.

Section 7-1: Downhill Lie Problem List

1. Golfers initially hit the ground behind their ball (they hit shots fat).
2. To avoid hitting shots fat, they often top or thin them.
3. As golfers are hitting fat/thin shots, they also struggle with their balance on their down- and through-swings.
4. After their best swings result in poorly struck, off-balance shots, they revert to "handsy" or "choppy" swings.

THE CAUSE OF THE PROBLEM

Almost all golfers learn their swings while standing on level golf mats or flat teeing grounds at their course or driving range. They learn essentially all of their swing mechanics and how to balance them-

selves while swinging on level, horizontal surfaces. Under these conditions they establish a consistent and repeatable "normal" swing arc, as shown in Figure 7-3A.

Unfortunately, all golf shots are not played off level hitting surfaces. So let's take our stick-figure golfer and his normal swing arc and ask him to hit a shot from a downhill lie (Figure 7-3B). In this situation, most golfers compensate for the downhill slope with their legs. They do this to keep their upper body feeling normal and their spine in a well-balanced vertical position.

Although they're aware of standing on a downhill slope, they adjust to the slope using their legs and knees. They don't take into consideration that the ground is sloping up behind their ball (Figure 7-3C). From their normal vertical body position and balance, they execute their normal swing, which hits the ground well behind the ball and flubs the shot. They don't realize that hitting off a downhill slope is similar to hitting from a level surface with a four-foot-long 2 x 6-inch board laid on its edge two feet behind their ball. If they don't do something to change their swing arc, the clubhead will hit the ground (or the board) behind their ball.

Figure 7-3: A normal swing from a near vertical position delivers the clubhead into the ground behind the ball.

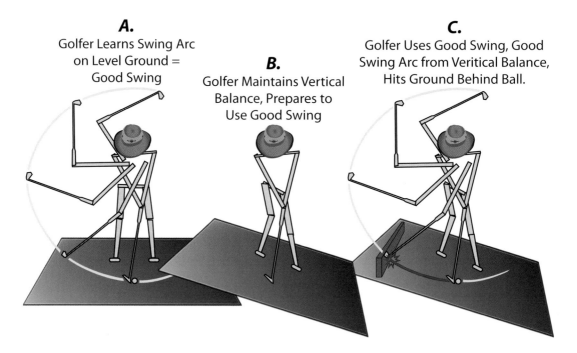

A.
Golfer Learns Swing Arc on Level Ground = Good Swing

B.
Golfer Maintains Vertical Balance, Prepares to Use Good Swing

C.
Golfer Uses Good Swing, Good Swing Arc from Veritical Balance, Hits Ground Behind Ball.

The Solution

It's not difficult to hit shots solidly from downhill lies. The pros do it all the time. But you can't hit them solidly using a normal swing arc while your upper body is vertically balanced relative to the slope. It just won't work.

What you need to do is to get your upper body and shoulders oriented perpendicular to the ground, just like you stand when you hit balls from a level (horizontal) lie. Then your normal swing will work. To do this, address the downhill shot as you normally would, then move your left foot 12 inches down the hill toward your target (X move in Figure 7-4). Using your left leg as a brace to stop you from losing your balance, lean your upper body (spine) toward the target until it becomes perpendicular to the ground (Y move in Figure 7-4). This will automatically tilt your shoulders (Z move in Figure 7-4) to mimic the downslope.

Figure 7-4: Downhill shots can be conquered if you adjust your setup properly.

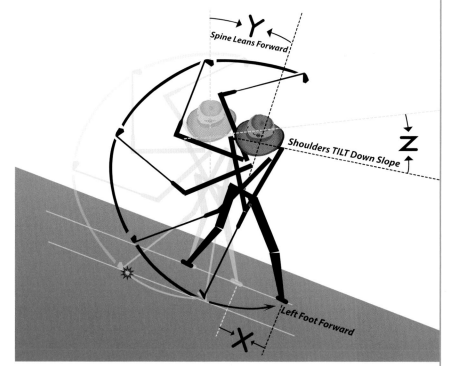

With your normal swing, the clubhead should now contact the ball before it hits the ground, without any hand or wrist manipulations. Be aware, however, that this setup will put great weight on your left leg and knee and cause you to lose your balance shortly after impact. To keep from falling you'll have to learn to walk "through" your downhill shots after impact.

How It Should Look

In short, you can solve your downhill dilemma by changing your setup, rather than trying to change your swing arc to avoid hitting behind the ball.

To understand how this shot should look, one must first learn a few simple fundamentals (no more stick-figure golfers). First, address the ball as if you were on a level playing surface, like I'm doing in my ghosted image in Figure 7-5A. Once you've aligned yourself

Figure 7-5A: The proper downhill stance: left foot forward, spine perpendicular to the ground, ball back in stance. (Note: The intuitive vertical stance you DON'T want is ghosted.)

correctly, move your left foot 12 inches down the hill toward the target. Next, lean your upper body and spine forward until both appear to be perpendicular to the ground. This will automatically move your hands ahead of the ball (Figure 7-5B) and establish your ball position well back in your stance, where it should be. Your hands should be well ahead of the ball.

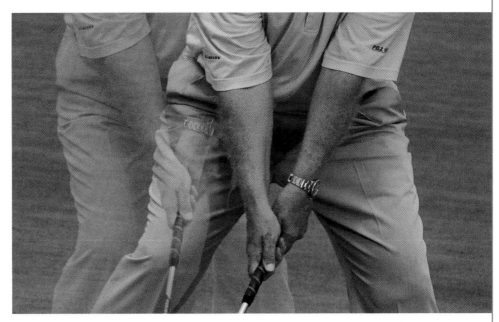

Figure 7-5B: When you step with your lead foot down the hill your grip doesn't change, but your hands and shaft move ahead of the ball.

Figure 7-6: Extra weight must be supported by your left leg and knee.

Be prepared for this setup to put about 80 percent of your weight on your forward leg. A number of years ago, when my knees were hurting me, I struggled to get into this position. I formed the habit of putting my hand on my left leg as I moved it down the hill, to help it get ready to accept the weight (Figure 7-6). Of course, you don't need to do this, but I do want you to realize that as you swing through impact, the weight on your left knee and leg will be extreme, so be ready for it.

Now, let's see how this shot looks from the Golfer's-Eye View (Figure 7-7). As you can see, the ball is clearly back in my stance (right-hand page) and my left leg is "loaded" and provides my downhill brace. Now rotate the book clockwise and look at the target (left page). Notice how beautiful this shot is, and how much trouble there is in front of and around the green. One more look down and then back again to the target as I waggle, and I'm ready to hit this downhill shot.

Figure 7-7: The Golfer's-Eye View to
Hole No. 9 at Hamilton Farm Golf Club.

All you have to do to pull this shot off successfully is to stay down and through the shot until after impact (Figure 7-8). For my six-foot-five frame, this was always easier said than done. If you examine this swing sequence carefully, you'll see that my head and shoulders stay with the slope of the terrain well through the fifth image. It's at this point that my left knee used to buckle because of the force on the knee, and I tended to come up and out of the shot before I got to this point. But thanks to my Steadman-Hawkins Institute knee surgery and rehab, I can now stay down through this shot and walk on through it after impact.

Figure 7-8: Stay down with the downhill shot through impact, then walk down the hill.

And of course, once you see the ball occasionally get up and on the green (Figure 7-9), it makes hitting these shots a whole lot more fun.

OPPOSITE: Figure 7-9: Anywhere on the green is a good shot for me from this downhill lie.

By the way, this hole is so visually stunning—and intimidating—that I wanted to show you the layup option available to the Hamilton Farm members (Figure 7-10). If my ball had not drawn a perfect lie or if my knees had been hurting, I would've definitely taken this safe route.

Figure 7-10: When a safe layup shot is available, you should consider playing it until you've practiced your downhillers. This is especially true if the next shot is a short wedge onto the green.

Additional Shot Options

WALKING THROUGH TO A ROCK

Now that you know how to set up successfully for a downhill shot, I'd like to show you a situation I found (see Figure 7-11) at Turning Stone Resort's Atunyote course in upstate New York. This shot is from a downslope, but it presents a different set of challenges than the previous shot shown. Not only does it require that I hit a solid shot to clear the water, but I must walk through the shot and onto a rock without falling into the lake.

Figure 7-11: Now *this* is a potentially hazardous downhill shot.

From the Golfer's-Eye View (Figure 7-12), this shot was a real beauty. Note my stance and how I had to brace my left foot up on the rock, which looks like a mountain here.

Figure 7-12: The downhill swing was difficult, but stopping my forward momentum on the rock was the biggest challenge for me.

Figure 7-13: This downhill shot was a bit rocky, but it sure was a lot of fun to hit.

The setup and swing required for this shot were no different from any other downhill shot I might face. The only thing I did differently than I normally would was my preparation for the shot. Before I actually tried to hit the shot, I took a number of slow-motion practice swings, gradually building up to the full-power swing I intended to use. As I gradually increased my swing power, I learned how I could step forward onto the rock without misstepping and falling. (I will admit, however, that I almost fell into the lake on one of the shots I hit from this lie (Figure 7-13). It was the closest I've ever come to dousing myself after hitting an on-course golf shot.)

Once you have a good feel for making downhill swings, I think you'll enjoy trying different ones, as I do now. When your fear and anxiety for a shot is gone and you have confidence that your swing technique can handle the situation, the game can take on a whole new perspective.

Of course, from this situation I was happy to see my shot land anywhere dry (Figure 7-14).

Figure 7-14:
Anywhere
on dry
land is
acceptable
from the
"Rock"

DOWNHILL IN THE SAND

If downhill sand shots terrify you, you're not alone. Many of our survey respondents described the shot in Figure 7-15, with some kind of danger (in this case, water) lurking behind the target, as the situation they feared most in golf. But please understand: The principles for hitting this shot are precisely the same as for hitting a downhill shot from the fairway.

Figure 7-15: A downhill sand shot toward water, with the green sloping away from me. A real nightmare shot.

The procedure for setting up is the same as that for a downhill lie in the grass. You set up as normal, move your left foot down the hill, and lean your upper body forward to get perpendicular to the slope (Figure 7-16). (Note: Because the camera was positioned slightly behind me in this photograph, the ball position does not appear to be as far back in my stance as it really is; the more severe the downslope, the farther back it should be.) My hands and shaft are again well ahead of the ball (inset photo), just as they were in the shots I hit earlier from the downhill grass lies.

Figure 7-16 and inset: For the downhill sand shot, move your lead foot down the slope, lean forward to get your upper body perpendicular to the sand, and let your hands move ahead of the ball.

Now look at this shot from the Golfer's-Eye View in Figure 7-17. The downhill sand shot toward water is a terrifying shot for many golfers, but it is also one of the most beautiful shots in the game. Give this photograph several rotations to see both your setup and the target, as if you were actually in my shoes and getting ready to play the shot. Would you be a little apprehensive about the outcome? I think most golfers would be.

Figure 7-17: The downhill sand shot toward water can be terrifying for many golfers.

From a wide stance with weight on my left leg, the ball back in my stance, and my upper body leaning forward, I was able to get the ball on the green without falling on my face (Figure 7-18).

Figure 7-18: In sand as in grass, the downhill shot is no walk in the park.

An absolute key to success with this shot is to stay down through and past impact. Notice how my shoulders and upper body remain perpendicular to the slope until the ball is well gone (frame 6).

Successful Examples

Phil Mickelson is the best I've ever seen at playing shots from down-hill lies, in part because he practices them. Here, for example, is a practice-round photo of Phil preparing several weeks before the 2009 U.S. Open at Bethpage Black golf course (Figure 7-19). Take note of how he leans forward on the downhill slope. As I recall, he hit shots from this area for about fifteen minutes during several different practice rounds. These shots aren't easy or very common-place, yet he practices them every chance he gets. Can you find slopes to practice on? If you can't, you may have to create them artificially in your own backyard.

Figure 7-19: Phil Mickelson practicing from the downslope behind the fourth green at Bethpage Black, site of the 2002 and 2009 U.S. Opens.

Figure 7-20: The view from behind Hazeltine's 10th green, looking back at the severely sloping fairway.

Figure 7-21: From a severe downslope, there's nothing easy about this pitching wedge shot to the 10th green at Hazeltine National.

I was deep into working on the downhill-shot section of this book when I happened to walk Hazeltine National Golf Club's short par-4 10th hole (ahead of the 2009 PGA Championship held there). I noticed the severe downhill lie that a golfer faces if his tee shot rolls just a little too far over the crest of the hill and onto the downslope of the fairway (Figure 7-20).

I walked up to the middle of that downslope to take a picture of the shot you face to the green if you bomb your drive and end up there (Figure 7-21). It's beautiful, but not for the faint of heart if you fear the downhill shot.

I found another example of how challenging a downslope can be as I walked an 18-hole practice round with a group that included talented young PGA TOUR pro Sean O'Hair. Eddie was lucky to catch this sequence (Figures 7-22 through 7-24) of his execution of the shot.

Figure 7-22: Sean O'Hair gets his feet set while still in his "vertical balance" posture.

Figure 7-23: O'Hair then leans forward, moving his shoulders toward the slope while bracing his weight with his left leg.

Figure 7-24: Sean stays down perfectly through impact and prepares to catch his balance.

Downhill sand shots when the ball is below your feet can be extra difficult to play. I even know of some TOUR professionals who don't particularly enjoy them. But we all have to deal with them, so we might as well get good at hitting them.

Conditioning Program

Your assignment now is to go to your backyard, create a downhill slope, and learn how to hit downhill shots from it. Why do I think you need backyard practice to conquer downhill shots? Because I don't believe you can find anywhere else to practice them at all, let alone practice them enough to overcome your fear of them!

I don't mean to pick on any particular golf course practice facility, but I think there is a problem with most of them. The game is played on all kinds of uneven surfaces (uphill, downhill, and side-hill slopes), but most practice facilities don't address these conditions. In all my years, I've never seen a flat golf course, but golfers are taught how to swing a club and play shots almost exclusively on beautiful, dead-flat practice tees—like the exquisite practice range at Hazeltine National (Figure 7-25) in Chaska, Minnesota.

By the way, if you ever get to the Vail, Colorado, area in the summertime, I had a neat feature built into the Dave Pelz Short

Figure 7-25: Hazeltine National's beautiful—but dead flat—practice tee.

Course at The Club at Cordillera. Each of the its holes presents you with the choice of level and uneven tee boxes (Figure 7-26). If you play from the uneven tees (Figure 7-27), you'll experience the uneven conditions that you find on most golf courses everywhere. And within every round there at Cordillera, I'm sure you'll find a few delightful downhill lies. Consider yourself invited to come to the Lodge and Spa at Cordillera and enjoy the golf!

Figure 7-26: You'll find uneven (left) and level (right, forward) tee boxes on hole No. 7 at Cordillera's Dave Pelz Short Course.

Figure 7-27: Another uneven tee box at Cordillera's Short Course.

NOW LET'S GET TO WORK

It's going to be simple for you to learn to hit downhill shots in your backyard. You don't need extensive equipment, just some al-mostGOLF balls, your wood-supported SYNLawn synthetic grass Fairway Mat, a few pieces of lumber, and your clubs. Start by laying your platform on a slight downhill slope, and get ready to start your practice (Figure 7-28).

Figure 7-28: My backyard practice tee (platform) on a slight downslope.

BACKYARD DRILLS

Step #1: For your first drill I recommend starting with a pitching wedge and hitting thirty almostGOLF balls to a laundry-basket target. Remember to set up before every shot with a routine to get your upper body perpendicular to, and your shoulders oriented parallel to, the ground (Figure 7-29). The following step-by-step checklist will help you do just that:

1. Address the downhill shot as you normally would on level ground: upper body vertical, ball centered in stance.
2. Move your left foot downhill and lean your upper body forward, toward your target, until your shoulders are parallel to the ground.
3. Stabilize your body in this position, bracing your weight with your left leg.
4. Waggle the club and look at your target twice; remind yourself to stay down through impact.
5. Hit the shot.
6. As you follow through, walk forward *through the shot* (toward the target) if your balance requires it.

Figure 7-29: On this slight downhill slope, I moved my left foot only three inches toward the target to achieve good balance.

Continue with the thirty-shot sessions to your target basket until you feel comfortable with your balance and your shot trajectory (Figure 7-30). Be aware that all shots from downhill lies fly lower than shots hit with the same club from level lies. Don't try to launch your shots higher using your hands and wrists, simply use a more-lofted club to compensate for the downhill loss of loft.

Figure 7-30: Practice until your balance is good after every shot.

Step #2: Insert plastic (or wood) spacers under the back side of your SYNLawn tee platform to increase the slope (Figure 7-31). It's important to make sure that your tee box is stable on the ground before you start to swing from it. Step carefully around every edge of the platform to locate any wobble or tilting due to your weight, and apply a shim between the platform and the ground where needed to make it completely solid.

Figure 7-31: The SYNLawn Fairway mat now has more downhill slope.

In Figure 7-31 I used a four-inch spacer under the back of the mat. The slope this produced forced me to move my left foot about 10 inches down the hill to get my shoulders parallel to the downslope and stabilize my balance.

Now you're ready to repeat your thirty-shot sessions until you again feel comfortable with your swing and balance on your follow-through. You may have to start stepping forward with a few little steps if your follow-through balance forces you to do so (Figure 7-32).

Figure 7-32: As the slope of the platform increases, it becomes more difficult to stay down through impact and catch my balance.

Step #3: Continue to increase the severity of the slope as you become more and more confident of your performance on each of the preceding slopes. With an eight-inch spacer under your platform, the downhill slope approaches the range of a 15 to 20 percent–grade downslope. At this slope, your shots will become seriously challenging to execute (Figure 7-33).

Figure 7-33: An eight-inch spacer under the back end of the platform begins to create real problems.

As you begin to practice on these increasingly steep lies, it's important that you're aware of how the downslope affects the launch height of your shots. As you can see in Figure 7-34, I've attached foam floaties to the faces of two wedges to indicate the normal loft angle of each club when held in their normal (as if on level ground) positions.

Figure 7-34: Foam floaties make the loft angles of a pitching and L-Wedge clearly visible (held as if on level ground).

But look at what happens to the "effective loft" of these wedges as I set up for a shot on this downhill lie (Figure 7-35). The reason why the effective loft changes so dramatically on downhill lies is that both the slope of the ground and the ball-back-in-stance and hands-forward address position subtract loft from the clubface at impact.

Figure 7-35: Both the downhill slope and hands-forward address decrease the effective loft of the wedges.

But don't worry! Your wide stance, coupled with your shoulders being tilted to the downslope, will make hitting these shots so much easier. And it's easy to go to a more-lofted club to compensate for lowering the effective loft at impact, as long as you're aware of the need for it.

This is not to say that playing shots from downhill lies will ever be easy. With every increase in downslope severity, your shots will become more difficult to launch in the air at an acceptable trajectory. It also becomes harder to stay down through the shot and catch your balance in your follow-through (Figure 7-36), both necessities for executing this shot properly.

Figure 7-36: Staying down through impact and keeping your balance are real problems on this downslope.

There is one more thing you need to remember: The skills required to stay down through impact and catch your balance become magnified when you generate more clubhead speed by making harder swings with longer clubs.

Once you can hit wedges from downhill lies, you are ready to move to longer clubs and longer golf swings. Step #4 in your practice regimen is to start with thirty-shot sessions on less severe downslopes and with longer clubs. Again, as your performance and confidence improve, progress to more severe slopes. When you feel you've got the setup, swing, and walk-through finish conquered with almostGOLF balls in your backyard, you're ready to go to the golf course.

TAKE IT TO THE COURSE

Your willingness to put time and effort into accomplishing your goals is what will make you successful in golf. You've started out being smart by learning the skills required to hit shots off downhill lies the easy way—with almostGOLF balls in your own backyard. There were no consequences for making bad swings and no lost strokes, and you were very time-efficient because of the at-home convenience. But now it's time to pick up the intensity a bit.

Hit a total of three hundred shots off downhill lies (thirty per session) with real golf balls off real grass lies. You need to have sessions with wedges, medium irons, long irons, and fairway woods (not the driver). To accomplish this you need to first find a golf course with an elevated practice tee. Elevation is required to provide a downhill slope from the front of the tee facing down to the range area. Then you need to find a time when no other golfers are hitting shots, so you can go onto the downslope at the front of the tee and practice (Figure 7-37) without putting yourself in danger.

Figure 7-37: Start with real balls on small slopes with wedges.

Now, I know this may be difficult to accomplish, and it certainly will be inconvenient at best, but I never promised it would be easy. From here on in it's up to you. If you want to conquer your fear of downhill shots, you need to find the facilities, devote the time, and do the groundwork. Move on to more and more severe slopes, and use longer clubs. Test yourself on the practice tee.

Seriously, it's better to learn during practice than to try to perform well while doing it for the first time, when your score depends on it. The bottom line is, if you follow this program, better play from downhill lies is there for the taking (Figure 7-38). Just take it!

OPPOSITE: Figure 7-38: Finish with longer clubs on more severe slopes as dusk approaches.

CHAPTER 8

③

Most Feared Shot #3:
Tight Lies

The Shot

THE PROS LOVE HITTING FULL shots off firm, fast fairways. In fact, they like tightly mown fairways so much that they often complain when the golf course doesn't play firm and fast. But they're not always as comfortable when they have to play short chip and pitch shots off a "tight" lie (Figure 8-1). And amateurs are downright terrified of these lies. To them, a wedge shot from a tight lie on firm ground is the third most feared shot in golf.

Of course, the definition of a tight lie varies from golfer to golfer. In working with many golf course superintendents, PGA TOUR players, and a full spectrum of amateurs over the years, I believe the consensus definition of a tight lie is one in which the ball sits within $1/8$-inch of a firm, hard surface beneath the grass.

Figure 8-1: This would be an easy wedge shot if the lie weren't so tight.

One must be careful when talking about tight lies because with a true tight lie, the distance between the bottom of the golf ball and the ground is less than either the length of the grass blades or the distance from the top of the grass to the ground. This is because a golf ball always sits down in the grass; it doesn't stay up on top of it. Golf course superintendents are exacting about how short they cut the grass, and they tell me they cut at ¼ of an inch (their mower height setting) to provide their members with tight lies in the fairway. Through my measurements, I've found that balls sit at least halfway down in such fairway grass and leave no more than an ⅛-inch cushion between the bottom of the ball and the dirt surface below.

If you think about this cushion distance, it will give you a clear understanding of why you fear tight lies. For the sake of clarity, when I refer to cushion distance I mean the actual distance between the bottom of the ball and the hard ground, regardless of what length the grass might be.

With this understanding, then, I will base the "tightness" of a lie on the cushion distance between the ball and the ground, as follows:

- ⅛ inch or less space is a tight lie
- ¼ inch is a perfect lie
- A ⅜-inch lie is a little too soft
- A ½-inch lie borders on fluffy (shots tend to hit high on the clubface and fall short of the target)

Any lie with a ¾ inch or more of cushion space is some classification of rough. If a ball is sitting up in such grass, it becomes very easy to hit under and produce a really bad shot.

The Problem

Figure 8-2: The visual definition of a really fat shot (also referred to as laying dirt or sod over the ball).

Golfers fear tight lies because they tend to hit so many fat (Figure 8-2) and skulled shots when faced with them.

After hitting shot after shot fat, golfers will do almost anything to not hit the next one fat. Of course, they then usually proceed to over-compensate and hit the next shot thin (Figure 8-3). Once a golfer's cycle of worry moves from fat to thin and back to fat again, they've started down a road toward anxiety and, not long thereafter, a fear of tight lies.

This fat/thin phenomenon is created by three unusual conditions that golfers face when hitting shots from tight lies on firm turf: 1) Their ball position is more critical than usual; 2) they are given much less margin for swing-level errors at impact; and 3) some wedges have too much bounce to allow successful shot execution from these circumstances. Let me explain these three conditions.

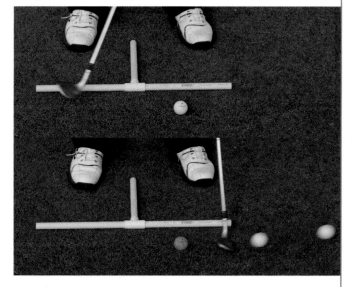

Figure 8-3: The visual definition of a skulled (i.e., thin) wedge shot.

BALL POSITION

The position of the ball in a golfer's stance—relative to the bottom of his swing arc—is an important aspect of any golf shot. But when the ball also sits on a tight lie, its placement becomes absolutely critical. In Figure 8-4, you'll see the toe view of a wedge passing through the bottom of its swing arc for a normal golf swing. The dashed black line traces its leading edge through this arc as it impacts several imaginary golf balls during an essentially perfect golf swing from a tight lie (assuming the club cannot penetrate the hard dirt below the ball). You can see that the clubhead contacts ball #2 just before it reaches the bottom of its arc, and club-ball contact occurs a little low on the clubface (although it's still a solid hit). This diagram represents a 60-degree wedge with modest bounce (bounce is a measure of the distance between the club's leading edge and the bottom of its sole). Notice what happens if that same perfect swing contacts ball #1 (ghosted), which is positioned two inches farther back in the player's stance. The leading edge skulls the shot (contact point marked by red star). Also notice that when the player addresses the ball a few inches farther

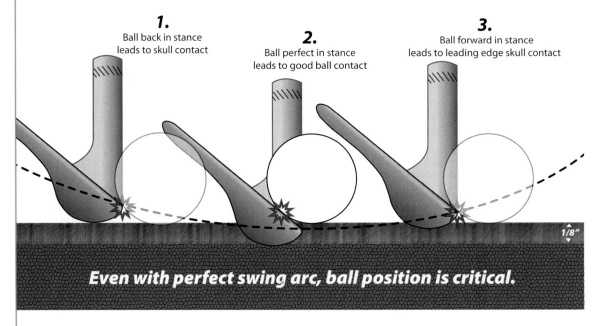

1.
Ball back in stance
leads to skull contact

2.
Ball perfect in stance
leads to good ball contact

3.
Ball forward in stance
leads to leading edge skull contact

1/8"

Even with perfect swing arc, ball position is critical.

Figure 8-4: Ball position is critical to hitting shots successfully off tight lies.

forward in his stance (ball #3, again ghosted), he is again rewarded with a skulled shot from the same perfect swing.

From this illustration you can see why ball position is so critical on tight-lie shots, and why it's so easy to hit skulled and thin shots in these kinds of situations.

PERFECT LIES PROVIDE GOOD MARGIN FOR SWING-LEVEL ERROR

Now imagine a professional golfer making three really good swings with his lob wedge at a ball sitting on a nice ¼-inch cushion of grass. All three swings have the same identical swing path except that on each succeeding swing, the bottom of his swing arc comes into the ball at a slightly lower level relative to the ground—as if he dipped his head or lowered his sternum slightly on each succeeding swing (Figure 8-5).

Both Figure 8-4 and the discussion above assume a normal position of a golfer's hands (slightly ahead of the clubhead) through impact. For many amateurs, however, the perfectly centered ball position might not be the best place for the ball on a tight lie. I'll deal with how to find the best ball position for your swing from tight lies in the conditioning section at the end of this chapter.

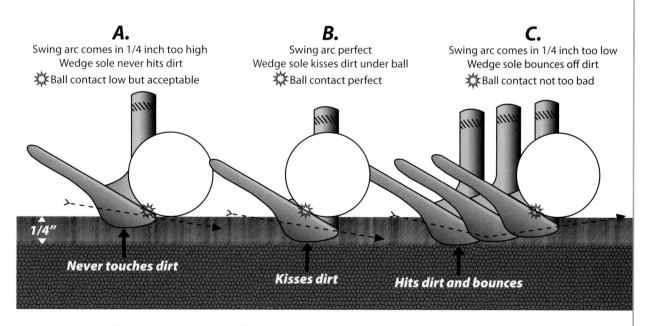

A.
Swing arc comes in 1/4 inch too high
Wedge sole never hits dirt
✸Ball contact low but acceptable

B.
Swing arc perfect
Wedge sole kisses dirt under ball
✸Ball contact perfect

C.
Swing arc comes in 1/4 inch too low
Wedge sole bounces off dirt
✸Ball contact not too bad

1/4"

Never touches dirt

Kisses dirt

Hits dirt and bounces

Figure 8-5: Illustration: The perfect lie is a ¼-inch grass cushion.

On swing A, our pro's swing is a little high up off the ground. The club clips only grass and never touches the dirt, and catches the ball low on the clubface. It's not perfect, but the shot flies acceptably. He says he hit the shot a little "thin," but he got away with it because the ball still made contact on the face of his wedge.

On his next swing (B), he lowers his swing arc slightly and his wedge kisses the dirt as it passes under the ball. This produces a perfect shot and he loves it.

On swing C, he lowers his swing arc slightly more again, which causes the sole of his wedge to hit the ground an inch behind the ball. The wedge bounces off the dirt and catches the ball a little low (but not too badly) on the clubface. He says he hit that shot a little heavy, but bounced into it and got away with it.

To summarize these three swings, all three produced fairly decent shots at slightly different distances, because the ¼-inch cushion lie provided enough margin for swing level error (above and below perfect) for all three shots to end up on the green.

TIGHT LIES GIVE ALMOST NO MARGIN FOR SWING-LEVEL ERRORS

Now look what happens if our pro makes the same three swings at a ball sitting in a tight lie with only a ⅛-inch cushion (Figure 8-6). On swing A, he brings his club into impact a little high (just like before) and the clubhead never hits the dirt. However, because of the tight lie, the leading edge of his L-wedge strikes the "belly" of the ball and skulls the shot. Swing B is slightly lower and his wedge kisses the dirt as he simultaneously catches the ball low on the clubface. Contact is very low on the clubface but it produces an acceptable shot result from this lie. However, when he brings his wedge in lower still, in swing C, his wedge hits the dirt behind the ball, bounces up into the ball, and he skulls another shot.

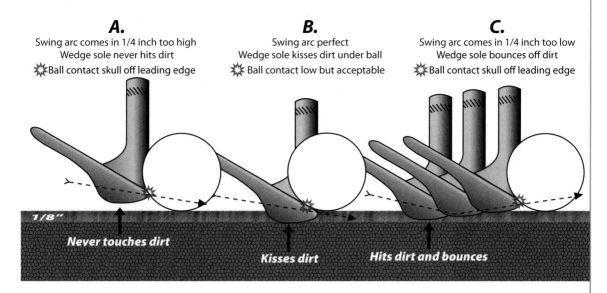

A.
Swing arc comes in 1/4 inch too high
Wedge sole never hits dirt
☀Ball contact skull off leading edge

B.
Swing arc perfect
Wedge sole kisses dirt under ball
☀Ball contact low but acceptable

C.
Swing arc comes in 1/4 inch too low
Wedge sole bounces off dirt
☀Ball contact skull off leading edge

1/8"

Never touches dirt

Kisses dirt

Hits dirt and bounces

Figure 8-6: Illustration: A tight lie with a ⅛-inch grass cushion provides little tolerance for swing-level errors.

To again summarize, the exact same three swings that produced one perfect and two very acceptable shots off ¼-inch-cushion perfect lies, produced one low (but playable) shot, plus two cold-skull zingers off ⅛-inch-cushion tight lies. The difference (or, more precisely, the lack of forgiveness) comes simply from the reduced space between the ball and the dirt.

The fact is, any golfer who has less than ⅛-inch variations in his swing level *should* fear tight lies. The tighter the lie, the smaller the margin for error, and the more reason for fear.

WEDGE BOUNCE IS CRITICAL

If a golf club had a sharp leading edge and a flat bottom, it would dig into the dirt like a shovel when the club struck the ground at a descending angle. This is why all clubs, but most important, wedges, have "bounce" built into the sole, or bottom, of the clubhead. When the sole of a wedge angles down and away from the leading edge, it causes the club to bounce off (instead of digging into) any ground that it hits.

The previous illustrations in Figures 8-4, 8-5, and 8-6 all show an L-wedge with only a modest amount of bounce protruding below its leading edge. This same 60-degree L-wedge (with modest bounce) can be used to hit perfect shots off tight lies if its sole can penetrate the dirt under the grass by an additional ⅛ of an inch. This would create the perfect cushion space of ¼-inch (⅛-inch grass + ⅛-inch dirt penetration = ¼-inch total cushion) below the ball, and produce a perfect shot (Figure 8-7: upper Swing A). Most normal turf will allow such penetration, but a tight lie on firm turf will not be as forgiving.

If the dirt below the tight lie is really hard, the wedge's sole can't penetrate it, so even on a perfect swing, contact with the ball will be made very low on the clubface, dangerously close to pro ducing a skulled shot (upper Swing B: ⅛-inch grass cushion only = contact low on the face).

But look what happens if a 55-degree sand wedge with a large amount of bounce is used for the same two shots (lower two clubs in Figure 8-7). To get decent contact even with a perfect swing (lower Swing A), the wedge would have to penetrate the soil by ¼ inch (which means the ground would have to be soft enough to let that happen). If the ground were really hard, as in lower Swing B, it would be impossible for the sand wedge to do anything but skull the shot.

A. 60° LOFT
Modest Bounce Normal Turf
Perfect contact, 1/8" grass cushion,
1/8" ground penetration.

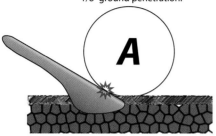

B. 60° LOFT
Modest Bounce Hard Turf
Dangerously low on face,
must have perfect swing.

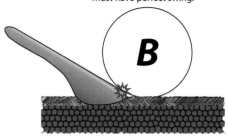

A. 55° WEDGE
Standard Bounce Normal Turf
Must have 1/4" perfect ground penetration necessary
to have a chance at good contact.

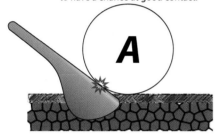

B. 55° WEDGE
Standard Bounce Hard Turf
No chance, Skull shot every time.

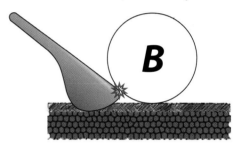

Figure 8-7: The degree of bounce on a wedge has a huge impact on how shots fly from tight lies.

The difficulty of hitting good shots off tight, firm lies is threefold:

1. Ball position is critical: If the ball is played either too far back or forward in the stance, bad shots will result.
2. The margin for swing-level errors is small: A golfer must swing his or her club's leading edge into impact at precisely the correct height to make solid contact.
3. Many golfers have too much bounce on their wedges, which prohibits good shots from tight lies.

The Solution

While I encourage you to conquer your fear of tight lies, I also want you to understand the truth of the situation: Tight lies are difficult shots to execute. Even the world's best players treat wedge shots from tight, firm lies with great respect. And even they will occasionally hit poor shots from these lies (yes, they are human). You must understand: It takes a precise strike with good ball position and proper equipment to hit a solid wedge shot from a tight lie. Shots from firm, tight lies are difficult to perform because they have the smallest tolerance for error of any of the ten most feared shots in golf. As a result, conquering this shot will take more patience and practice time from you than any of the other most feared shots.

Having said that, let me give you a road map for developing the skills you need to conquer this shot. Tight lies *can* be conquered (many golfers have proven this), and having the confidence to play tight lie shots under pressure is a wonderful skill to have in this game.

BALL POSITION

First, you must learn to position the ball precisely in your stance every time you set up to hit a shot from a tight lie (Figure 8-8). For most swings this position will be at or behind the center of the stance, midway between the ankles. In our schools, we use a T-Square to make sure this position is clearly visible and obvious during practice.

Figure 8-8: The perfect tight-lie ball position for most swings.

SWING LEVEL

Once you've gotten your ball position correct, you must learn to control your swing arc—to consistently keep the level of the bottom of your swing arc at the proper height relative to the ground as it approaches the ball. This means that the leading edge of your wedge must approach tight-lie shots at precisely the right height every time. This is by far the most difficult part of learning to hit good shots from tight lies. To maintain a consistent swing-arc level, you must keep your head and sternum (the swing center of your body) level, and the radius of your swing (the distance between your sternum and the ball) should be the same at impact as it was at address. Keeping this radius constant requires a firmness within your left arm (for right-handed golfers) throughout the swing.

WEDGE BOUNCE

And finally, if you don't have a wedge with *at least* 60 degrees of loft and a small amount of bounce, get one! A high-bounce sole forces the leading edge of the club up off the ground. Only if you have a low bounce wedge can you slide its leading edge between the ball and the turf to produce good trajectory shots from firm, tight lie conditions.

How It Should Look

BALL POSITION

As I stated earlier, for most golfers the best ball position for tight-lie shots will be the center of their stance. To find your stance center, look at your ankles, not your toes. Your left toe (lead foot for right-handed golfers) should be flared toward the target to offer less resistance against the rotation of your lower body through impact. But while flaring your lead toe toward the target is good, it can also make the ball appear to be farther back in your stance than it really is. Look carefully at Figure 8-9: You'll see that if I squared my left foot—instead of leaving it flared toward the target—my ball would be centered between my ankles.

Also notice that my hands are slightly forward of a line between my head and the ball (Figure 8-9). Remember this and use it in your swing because your hands must always stay ahead of the clubhead through impact (with a slightly forward shaft lean, as in Figure 8-9 inset), on tight-lie shots. If your clubhead passes your

Figure 8-9: The perfect ball position for most golfers is centered between the ankles, with hands slightly ahead of the ball (inset).

hands prematurely (prior to impact), the leading edge will start moving upward, away from the ground, and produce a skulled shot. The way to keep your hands ahead of the clubhead through impact is to make sure the length of your backswing is shorter than your follow-through. In our schools we call this swinging from short (backswings) to long (follow-throughs). Remember: On tight lies, swing "short to long"!

SWING LEVEL

Now look at my swing in Figure 8-10, and notice how I keep my head level (or still) from address until about halfway into my follow-through. You'll also see that my left arm (while not tense or tight) stays completely extended to establish a constant radius for my swing arc. Both of these moves are key to achieving a level swing arc with consistency.

Figure 8-10: A stable head position and a constant left-arm radius create a level swing arc.

WEDGE BOUNCE

To see how Phil Mickelson sets up to hit shots from tight lies, examine the close-up in Figure 8-11. He lays the face of his 64-degree wedge wide open, so you can imagine the leading edge sliding in low enough to the ground to allow the clubface to contact the ball. Phil grinds the sole under the heel of his wedge (as many TOUR players do) to allow the club to lay open without raising the leading edge up off the ground.

Figure 8-11: To hit shots from tight lies, Phil Mickelson lays his wedge face wide open.

Figure 8-12: Mickelson's wedge kisses the turf on tight-lie pitch shots.

Phil is the best I've ever seen at this shot. After sixty shots (I counted them) he had taken only two divots from the firm, tight turf at Augusta National Golf Club's practice range (Figure 8-12), while lofting every ball nicely to his target. His wedge kept kissing the turf below each ball: no fat shots, no skulled shots, not even a heavy or thin shot. The precision and skill he has developed in keeping the level of his swing arc consistent is impressive.

Now imagine you're ready to hit the 60-yard wedge shot in Figure 8-13. Center the ball between your ankles, as demonstrated on the right-hand page of the Golfer's-Eye View photo, then look at your target (left-hand page; rotate book clockwise 45 degrees and tilt head left). Look back at the ball (right page), then back to the target again as you imagine yourself waggling the club (left page).

Figure 8-13: Golfer's-Eye View: Make sure the ball position is perfect, then think "level as she goes."

As you waggle (twice), think of your swing keys: head still, swing radius constant, level swing arc. Then go. Make your best swing and you've done it; you've just hit a perfect 60-yard wedge shot from a tight lie (Figure 8-14). And as I said at the beginning of this chapter, how does it get much better than that?

Figure 8-14: Incoming wedge shots from tight lies tend to have a lot of spin on them.

An Additional Shot Option

If you're not comfortable hitting a full or partial wedge shot off a tight lie, there is another option: the bump-and-run shot. It's an easier shot to hit because it has a greater margin for swing level error than a wedge shot from the same lie. That's the good news. The bad news is that you can't control its direction or distance as accurately as a well-struck wedge, because the ball must bounce and roll along the ground on an unknown surface. Also, there will be times where you can't aim a bump-and-run shot at your target because of water, a sand trap, or another obstacle that's in the way.

To hit a standard bump-and-run shot, begin by gripping down a few inches on your 6-iron (Figure 8-15 and inset).

Figure 8-15: Setup for a bump-and-run shot.

The bump-and-run shot requires the same principles as hitting a wedge from a tight lie, but there is much more room for error in its execution. You still want to have the ball centered in your stance (Figure 8-16, between your ankles, not your toes), and you need to create a level swing arc. By gripping down on the shaft you'll make the club a little shorter so you won't hit the shot too far. And as with the wedge, you want to keep your hands slightly ahead of the ball through impact.

Figure 8-16: Ball position is less critical with a bump-and-run shot, but the ball should still be near the center of your stance with your hands slightly forward.

Your bump-and-run swing should be somewhat of a sweeping motion (Figure 8-17). There is no need to take a divot. Remember, the grass is short and the turf is firm. Forget about swinging hard and generating any extra backspin; all you want to do is roll the ball to your target.

Figure 8-17: Your bump-and-run swing should sweep the ball off the ground.

I suggest that you learn to hit bump-and-run shots even if you become an excellent wedge player from tight lies. You never know when you're going to need this shot, and it's not that hard to learn. But you do need to have some feel for how big a swing to make for any given shot. It's actually quite fun to practice and play with the bump and run. And who knows, with the USGA changing rules to allow less backspin from wedge shots, the bump and run may become even more valuable in the future.

Conditioning Program

I find it interesting that tight lies are different than many of the other feared shots in this book. Some of them require significant intellectual learning and the understanding of four or five new skills before you can really begin to play them well. But after that, the physical repetition and learning are fairly simple. For example, learning to escape from buried lies in sand is much easier once you understand how everything works between the ball, club, and sand.

On the other hand, to conquer tight lies you only need to get a low-bounce wedge and learn where to play the ball in your stance. The rest is all swing work and repetition. But it takes quite a bit of time to groove your swing level to the required precision level.

So let's get started on learning the most difficult shot to conquer in this book. I'll give you a road map (it's almost a straight road of progressively more difficult drills) for developing the skills you need to hit the shot, and then it will be up to you to spend the time, patience, and energy to accomplish the task.

IN YOUR BACKYARD

The three keys to hitting good shots from tight lies are:

1. Use a low-bounce wedge.
2. Establish the best ball position for your swing.
3. Develop the ability to swing with a consistently level swing arc.

STEP #1: GET READY TO PLAY SOME BOARD GAMES

The only equipment you need is your low-bounce wedge, ten almost-GOLF balls and three, 4-foot-long, 2" x 6" boards. Your first task will be to hit twenty-four pitch shots (30 yards is sufficient) from one board while standing on the other two (Figure 8-19). But don't hit any shots yet. I want you to first determine the best ball position in your stance for your swing on tight lies.

Figure 8-19: Set up to your ball on the board as you would a tight lie in grass.

STEP #2: LEARN HOW BALL POSITION AFFECTS YOUR WEDGE'S LEADING EDGE

Yes, setting your ball directly on a piece of wood leaves zero cushion below the ball, but that's exactly what we need for now. Before you spend time hitting shots for your first drill, you need to learn how your ball position affects the position of your wedge's leading edge through impact. This understanding will help you determine which ball position will work best for your swing.

First examine a series of ball positions relative to *my* stance (you'll examine your own in your backyard). I'm going to show you how the leading edge of my low-bounce, 64-degee X-Wedge moves up and down, relative to where it contacts the ball, depending on where I position the ball in my stance. I'll start by addressing a ball in exactly the center of my stance (Figure 8-20), with my hands in an impact position slightly ahead of the club-head. Look carefully and you'll see that the leading edge of my wedge is raised only a little off the wood, but that's enough to make contact with the ball. This is not good, and would result in a very low trajectory shot at best. More than likely, it would be a thin or slightly skulled shot.

Now look what happens if I move the ball forward in my stance two inches (Figure 8-21A). The leading edge of the wedge moves up just a fraction, probably enough to make me hit a thin or skulled shot with any swing I make. And this is with my lowest-bounce wedge. Imagine what would happen if I had more bounce on the sole of this club! In that case, I would have no chance to loft balls off this wooden platform lie.

But we're learning here, so let's keep on going. Next look what happens when I move the ball another two inches forward in my stance. This puts the ball four inches forward of center and again raises the leading edge of my wedge a little higher. There is no question from this position that the leading edge would cause a skulled shot (Figure 8-21B).

Figure 8-20: With the ball in the center of my stance, the leading edge might skull the shot.

Figure 8-21A: With the ball two inches forward of center, the leading edge is even more likely to skull the shot.

Figure 8-21B: With the ball four inches forward of center in my stance, there's no doubt the leading edge will skull every shot.

If you're thinking at this point that you might be wasting time—because you're probably not going to be hitting off wooden surfaces very often—think again. This toe view of what happens to a wedge's leading edge when the ball is sitting on a hard wooden surface is very instructive. If we were looking at the same phenomenon in grass, it would be very difficult to see these differences and what was actually going on with the club's leading edge. And besides that, you *will* be hitting shots off the wooden plank in your backyard (and off hard-packed dirt on the golf course) before this is over.

Figure 8-22: With the ball positioned one inch back of center in my stance, the leading edge should miss it entirely.

You can see by now that moving the ball forward in your stance is not a good thing to do when your lie is tight. So let's go the other way and move the ball back in my stance one inch behind center and see what happens (Figure 8-22). Clearly the leading edge is significantly lower, and ball contact will probably occur on the clubface. Now we're making progress!

Figure 8-23: With the ball another two inches back of center, my swing arc becomes the issue, not wedge bounce.

And when we move the ball back another two inches in my stance, the leading edge has moved lower still (Figure 8-23). But now the clubface has become significantly delofted. Also, the ball looks so far back in my stance that I'm beginning to worry if I can get my swing arc low enough to the ground to avoid skulling the shot.

Figure 8-24: I do best from tight lies with the ball one inch back of stance center and my clubface slightly open.

At this point, I think you know that where you play the ball in your stance has a significant influence on how high the leading edge comes up off the ground. And I want to give you my experience with this phenomenon. I have experimented with hitting shots from many tight lies with my own swing and reached this conclusion: When I play the ball one inch behind center in my stance *and* open my clubface fractionally to the right (which allows my wedge to sit down just a little lower on its heel; see Figure 8-24), I hit my best shots from tight lies.

This is the end of intellectualizing about ball position. It's now time for you to hit ten almostGOLF balls (off wood) from each of the ball positions I have shown you above and see which ball position gives you the best results. Use your normal wedge swing. After hitting ten shots each from the five ball positions pictured, try to determine if there is one that you prefer. If you're torn between two positions, hit ten more shots from each and repeat if necessary. You need to come out of this test with a favorite ball position for your most lofted low-bounce wedge when hitting from a supertight lie on solid wood.

Now switch to real golf balls and hit ten shots off the wooden board. Experiment with small changes in ball position around the one you chose from your previous testing. I think you'll enjoy this testing, and you may even be a little surprised at how easily you can hit reasonably lofted shots with no cushion below the ball (once you get your ball position and wedge bounce right). But now let's take a break.

THE BUMP AND RUN

Figure 8-25: Hitting a bump-and-run shot with a 6-iron virtually eliminates any chance of skulling the ball.

Let's see why the bump-and-run shot is a viable option from a tight lie. If you look at Figure 8-25, it should be clear that there is no way I can skull my 6-iron from this setup unless my clubhead comes up off the ground by almost an inch. When you play a bump-and-run shot you essentially take the possibility of skulling the shot off the table. You can still hit this shot fat, but if you've been able to keep your swing level constant, you should have no problems hitting the ball solidly.

STEP #3: START GROOVING YOUR TIGHT-LIE SWING

It's now time to start grooving your tight-lie swing. Get a laundry basket and set it 30 yards from your platform as your target. Hit twenty-four shots with almostGOLF balls and another twenty-four with real golf balls to your basket (Figures 8-26 and 8-27). This forty-eight-shot exercise

Figure 8-26: Hit lofted shots from a wood platform with almostGOLF balls.

Figure 8-27: A real ball flies about the same as an almostGOLF ball off wood.

counts as one session's worth of swings (about thirty minutes of time); make sure to keep track of how many of these forty-eight shots you hit poorly. Repeat this session four times a week in your backyard until you record two consecutive sessions with zero skulled shots. When you accomplish this, you're ready for the next step in your tight-lie training.

MOVE ONTO DIRT (HARD DIRT)

The next step is to continue to refine your tight-lie swing by moving onto some real dirt. You're actually quite likely to encounter hard-dirt lies on the golf course, but the real reason to practice off dirt is that it's actually much more difficult to hit good shots from this surface (Figure 8-28) than it is from wood (slightly fat shots are worse from dirt if any *material* gets between the clubface and the ball). This is the direction you need to go with your training, because the more difficult the lie, the tighter the tolerance for error. Hitting from dirt will give you better feedback for making better swings off tight lies.

Figure 8-28: Try your tight-lie swing off hard-packed dirt (also known as "hardpan").

From dirt lies you should again hit twenty-four balls each with almostGOLF and real balls until you execute two perfect sessions—this time with no fat or skulled shots—in a row. Getting past the dirt drill may take you longer than perfecting the wood drill because it's very easy to hit fat shots off dirt lies. Regardless of how long it takes (days, weeks, months), keep swinging on dirt lies until your swing level is good enough to hit forty-eight good pitch shots twice in a row. You will need the confidence in your swing that this drill can bring, because things are going to get even more difficult.

THE FINAL PHASE OF BACKYARD GROOVING

For the final drill, we constructed a special platform with a container in it to hold sand and water (you can make one on your own). This drill is a difficult one that focuses on keeping your swing arc level. The object is to hit 30-yard pitch shots from a clean lie in sand by picking the ball cleanly off the surface (Figures 8-29 and 8-30). This shot is much more difficult than it looks, because if your swing level is a little low you'll hit too much sand behind the ball and the shot will go nowhere. But if your swing level is a little high, you'll skull the shot.

All I ask is that you repeat this drill five times, hitting forty-eight shots each time (as in the sessions above). You could also do this at your golf course if they have a practice sand bunker.

Figure 8-29: It's not easy to pick the ball cleanly off sand.

Figure 8-30: Picking the ball cleanly from sand will help develop a constant swing level.

Then I want you to try the same drill again, except this time, hit forty-eight shots off the surface of water. This drill is really fun but extremely difficult. We filled our platform container two inches deep with water and cut some two-inch-long plastic tubes to use as underwater tees. This allowed us to set our golf balls precisely on top of the water (Figure 8-31), just as in the previous drill when we hit balls that were resting on sand.

Please understand, I'm not asking you to hit these shots to punish you (although they really are difficult). I want you to have some success with these drills so that when you get to the golf course and face tight lies with only a ⅛-inch cushion of grass beneath them, they will seem *easy* compared to what you've been facing.

Figure 8-31: The ultimate challenge: to pick the ball cleanly off water.

That's it for your backyard training. Now you can go to the golf course and play the game. If your course has a good short-game area, you might find some tight lie shots to practice there. But if they are good lies on normal fairway grass, they'll have too much cushion beneath the ball to really challenge you. You'll have to wait until you catch the occasional tight lie out on the course for your ultimate challenge. If you followed our conditioning program as detailed above, however, you'll be ready for it.

Good luck, and give yourself some love—feel good and enjoy it—the next time you hit a good shot from a tight lie!

CHAPTER 9

Most Feared Shot #2:
Greenside Sand

2

The Shot

SAND BUNKERS MAKE GOLF COURSES LOOK BEAUTIFUL. At the same time, they make the game more challenging and rewarding in terms of shot values (Figure 9-1), especially for the average golfer.

I know you've probably heard TOUR professionals say, "I love the sand. I'd rather be in the sand than in the surrounding rough." But not many of our survey golfers felt that way. In fact, they voted the greenside bunker shot the second most feared shot in golf.

Figure 9-1: A greenside bunker shot with water behind the flag.

Why? Because only golfers who are good at getting out of sand think a greenside sand shot is easy. They know they'll hit a reasonably good shot when they get into sand, and have full confidence in playing from it. The golfer who fears sand, however, expects poor results as he approaches a greenside bunker, doesn't understand what a good sand swing should feel like, and almost never practices the shot. To the sand-fearing golfer, sand is a four-letter word.

And our survey golfers weren't talking about extra-difficult plugged lies in the sand, awkward stances or shots with superlong carries over dangerous trouble areas. Their fear was of hitting an ordinary greenside bunker shot from a good lie, the kind the TOUR pros are often thinking about holing. Give many amateurs a perfect lie with the ball sitting on top of nicely raked sand . . . and they're scared to death!

The Problem

There are a lot of reasons to fear a shot from sand if the swing isn't being executed properly. In fact, I think I could write an entire book on things that have happened to golfers I know personally in the sand. For example, when a player's clubhead hits too far behind the ball, or digs down too deeply into the sand, it loses too much speed (power) to successfully move the ball up and out of the sand (Figure 9-2). Even when the ball does come out under this scenario, it either doesn't carry far enough to reach the green, or it bounces and rolls too far when it hits the green, because it was launched with little or no backspin.

After leaving their fair share of fatted shots in the sand, golfers usually get mad at them-

Figure 9-2: Taking too much sand behind the ball.

selves and vow to avoid a similar result the next time they walk into a greenside bunker. This vow usually results in a shot that screams into the bunker lip or sails over the green, because the ball was thinned or bladed (Figure 9-3) by a wedge that never entered (or even touched) the sand.

Wanting desperately to get out of the sand but not knowing how to do it is a terrible combination for a golfer. Especially when they also have fear, and fearful reactions, in their mind and body. This set of circumstances runs rampant in the world of amateur golf,

Figure 9-3: A skulled sand shot often follows several fat ones.

and creates fear (sometimes progressing into stark terror) in the hearts of those who find their ball lying in the sand.

Take a look at the cold, hard data in Figure 9-4, which certainly justifies amateurs' fears of the sand. This data comes from our PGA

Figure 9-4: Up-and-down percentage from greenside sand versus USGA Handicap Index.

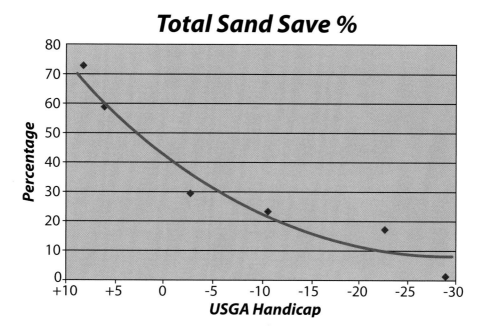

TOUR/ShotLink and Pelz Golf Institute research teams—gathered over three years from serious amateur golfers playing under tournament conditions (The GOLF.com World Amateur Handicap Championship; www.worldamgolf.com). Every bunker shot in this database was made with great focus by the amateurs in an attempt to get the ball close to the hole.

Look how the up-and-down percentage (the percentage of shots holed in two strokes or less from the bunker) drops from the average TOUR player (+5.5 on the USGA Handicap system) to the 3-handicap golfer, and then to the higher handicappers. If you are a 30+ handicap golfer, you probably don't know what getting up-and-down out of a bunker feels like. Imagine your excitement when you actually achieve an up-and-down out of a greenside bunker! (For all you detail hounds, the leftmost data point in Figure 9-4 is the 2009 PGA TOUR player best (Luke Donald) sand save percentage of 64%.)

GOLFERS DON'T KNOW WHAT TO DO IN THE SAND

Most amateurs who fear the sand either don't know the fundamentals of good sand technique, or else they think they know them but really *don't*. They have developed a fear of sand play based on a variety of failed results and reasons.

Some golfers think they have to make a special "sand trap" swing, without really knowing what that means. Others don't know where the ball should be positioned in their stance or if the clubface should be laid open or kept square in the sand. And most don't realize that pros use essentially the same swing motion for sand shots as they do for their three-quarter wedge shots from grass.

Particularly damaging to a golfer's psyche is if they think they know how to get out of the sand, but then struggle with the shot's execution.

The Solution

To hit a good greenside bunker shot, you must not play the ball back in your stance or hit shots with a square clubface, and you shouldn't create a special swing just to get out of the sand.

BALL POSITION

If the ball is positioned too far back in your stance, the clubhead is likely to enter the sand too close to the ball (even with a good swing) and hit more ball than sand. To avoid that result, a back-in-stance ball position requires you to fall back on your downswing to hit the sand far enough behind the ball (Figure 9-5).

Figure 9-5: A ball positioned too far back in your stance requires a "fall-back" swing to hit behind it.

FACE ALIGNMENT: OPEN VS. CLOSED

Even when everything else goes well for a golfer, if the leading edge of the club is positioned squarely to its path—like the angle of a shovel as it enters the sand—it will dig down into the sand and ruin the shot (Figure 9-6).

DON'T CREATE A "SPECIAL" SAND SWING

The same basic wedge swing you use successfully from grass will work wonderfully from sand if you follow two principles: 1) Position your ball some four to five inches forward of normal in your stance, and 2) Lay the face of your wedge open.

The arc of your normal wedge swing makes contact with the ball at the center of your stance in grass, and then bottoms out about four inches forward of that (as it creates a divot). You should position your ball in the sand four to five inches forward of where you normally play it in grass. This will allow

Figure 9-6: A square clubface (top) digs like a shovel, while an open clubface (bottom) bounces off the sand.

your wedge to naturally enter the sand well behind the ball, exactly where it normally contacts the ball in grass. If you have laid the face of your wedge open—so that the club's sole is exposed to the sand before the leading edge—the clubhead will bounce off the sand, sliding under and past the ball to "blast" it out of the sand.

The solution to good sand play is to:

1. Play the ball forward in your stance.
2. Lay the clubface of your wedge open (to the right) as you aim slightly to the left.
3. Use your normal wedge swing aggressively.

How It Should Look

RULES FOR BLASTING FROM GOOD LIES IN THE SAND:

- ► Align your feet, body, and swing line left (about three steps) of the flagstick.
- ► Play the ball forward in your stance, opposite your left instep (relative to swing line).
- ► Open your clubface 45 degrees while keeping your hands in their normal grip position.
- ► Make your normal wedge swing from grass—three-quarter backswing, full follow-through.
- ► Maintain the same wrist cock and swing rhythm as your normal three-quarter wedge swing.
- ► Produce a sand divot that is shallow and long (clubhead scoots under and past ball).
- ► Accelerate the clubhead through impact so that it initially travels twice as far as the ball.

I want you to look at and internalize these rules and relationships one at a time.

SETUP IS FIRST

If you can't set up in sand . . . you can't play from sand.

How you set up to a greenside bunker shot is crucial. If you want to consistently get the ball out of the sand and onto the green in one shot, you must start with a good setup and leave your swing mechanics for later.

AIM FEET, BODY, AND SWING LINE LEFT; AIM CLUBFACE SLIGHTLY RIGHT OF THE FLAGSTICK

Look from above and behind the golfer in Figure 9-7. Examine each arrow carefully and think about how you're going to do this. Stand up right now (as you hold this book), wherever you are, and imagine setting up to hit a sand shot, with your TV set as your target pin. You must understand this alignment relationship and remember it before you'll ever learn to play well from sand.

Figure 9-7: View from above: yellow = swing line (aim line); red = feet/body line (parallel to aim line); white = target line (flagstick)

From a down-the-line view, study the exact same setup and alignment positions during an actual swing (Figure 9-8).

Figure 9-8: Ty Waldron, a senior instructor in our Dave Pelz Scoring Game Schools, demonstrates the sand blast from a good lie in the bunker.

FORWARD BALL POSITION, OPEN CLUBFACE

Now, examine how your forward ball position should look when you stand over your shot in the sand and look down (Figure 9-9). Notice that we've added the same lines from Figure 9-7 to our Golfer's-Eye View image to help you correlate your left-instep ball position with the direction of your body alignment (red line) and swing path (yellow line) relative to the target line (white line). Also notice how open the clubface looks as you align it a little right of the flagstick.

Figure 9-9: The Golfer's-Eye View of a proper setup in sand.

MAKE YOUR NORMAL WEDGE SWING FROM GRASS IN THE SAND

The proof of how well a normal wedge swing can work in the sand is demonstrated by my good friend Steve Elkington in Figure 9-10 below. Elks' sand game is exceptional. As you can see, his swings from the grass and the sand are close to being identical.

You can also see that Elk's wrist cock and swing rhythm in sand are almost mirror images of his normal three-quarter wedge swing from grass. Of course, the ball flies much farther when he hits it from grass than it does when he scoots his open-faced club under it in the sand.

Most golfers who struggle in sand set up poorly, and then worry about their swing mechanics. When you start from a bad position, it's like tying one hand behind your back when you're hanging wallpaper. There's not much your swing can do to save you.

Figure 9-10AB: Steve Elkington plays from grass (A) and sand (B) with the same swing motion.

YOUR DIVOT IN SAND SHOULD BE
LONG AND SHALLOW

Your sand divot should be very shallow (about ¾-inch deep) and maybe 10 inches long (not the splash, just the divot). These dimensions are not exact or particularly important, since different-length shots and types of sand behave differently. But the point is that you definitely don't want to create short or deep divots.

THE CLUBHEAD INITIALLY TRAVELS TWICE THE
DISTANCE AND SPEED OF THE BALL AFTER IMPACT

Your clubhead must not slow down as it scoots underneath and past your ball. By making an aggressive forward swing and following through to a nice full finish, you can keep your club moving rapidly under and past the ball. This will impart backspin to the shot and provide control to stop the ball once it hits the surface of the green.

Notice how well Phil Mickelson keeps his wedge accelerating past the ball (Figure 9-11) during his preparation for the 2009 U.S. Open at Bethpage Black golf course on Long Island. You can clearly see that his clubhead travels twice the distance of his ball initially after impact.

Figure 9-11: Phil Mickelson during preparation for the 2009 U.S. Open at Bethpage Black.

Study this swing and imagine yourself looking like that when you play from sand. The more you internalize Phil's and Elk's sand motions into your brain, the better you will play from sand.

An Additional Shot

You don't always have to blast balls out of the sand. You can chip or even putt them if the ball is sitting cleanly on top of the sand and the bunker lip is very low. If you putt across sand, it should be firm or a little wet and there must be no lip to the edge of the bunker.

Figure 9-12:
When there is
no lip, putting
might be
the easiest
way out.

In a photo shoot I did for *GOLF Magazine*, I demonstrated putting out of a bunker with no lip (Figure 9-12). In terms of "knowing your own game" and hunting the lowest score, amateurs with bunker issues don't always have to go directly at the flagstick (for

example, in this instance, with water behind the hole). In this circumstance I might recommend that they putt the ball up onto the fringe and take their chances of two-putting from there. This would eliminate any possibility of hitting the ball into the water. I encourage you to always check your options from the bunker until you've developed full confidence in your blast shot.

Success Examples

You've now seen how to set up for a greenside bunker shot. And no, don't try to complicate things by worrying about where your weight or shoulders should be, or how tight or loose your grip pressure should be. Use your normal wedge motion and swing aggressively.

Hopefully, you've internalized your vision of what a good sand swing should look like. But I emphasize that just knowing how to get out of the sand is not enough. I don't want to discourage you, but *all* players must take the time to practice and groove their sand swings if they want to play consistently well from sand. Once you've learned the swing fundamentals and how to set up, frequent repetition is the key.

The best sand players I know practice their sand swings all the time. Steve Elkington (Figure 9-10), D.A. Weibring (Figure 9-13) and Phil Mickelson (Figures 9-14, 9-15, 9-16) all practice diligently, session after session, tournament

Figure 9-13: D.A. Weibring practicing his bunker technique at the 2009 Players.

after tournament, to groove their sand games. Some days they work on their rhythm or ball position, other days they work on fine-tuning their precision entry points behind the ball.

Figure 9-14: Phil Mickelson practicing from the sand at the 2007 PGA Championship.

Figure 9-16: Lefty from the practice-area pot bunker at the 2007 Open Championship.

Figure 9-15: More practice for Phil at the 2008 Masters.

Conditioning Process

Now that you know how important it is to set up properly, it's time to work on your swing execution.

If your wedge doesn't enter the sand in approximately the same place every time, or penetrate the sand to about the same depth every time, you'll always struggle with your greenside bunker shots. You must be able to control the club's entry point and the depth it travels through the sand. In every school we teach, we instruct our students to train both their minds and bodies to do just this.

Our favorite conditioning drill for creating a consistent sand divot (consistent entry point plus consistent divot depth) is the "Line Drill" (Figure 9-17ABCD). The truth is, all you have to do to hit a good sand shot is produce the proper-sized sand divot under your ball. Your clubface never touches the ball anyway, so the whole point of a good sand swing is to create a good sand divot in the right place under your ball.

LINE DRILL

Before you perform this drill, you need a thorough understanding of how to set it up and execute it properly. To set up for the Line Drill, you first draw a line in the sand extending out away from your left instep, which represents your normal ball position in the sand. Then you place five balls on that line. Next, you draw a second entry-point line approximately five inches (almost three ball-widths) behind your ball-position line (Figure 9-17A). This is the point where you want the bottom of your wedge clubhead to first touch the sand. As you practice this drill, you can pretend there's an imaginary ball resting on your entry-point line and try to hit it with your normal wedge swing (as if you were hitting from grass), except that

Figures 9-17A and 9-17B: After setting up the Line Drill (left), my first practice swing enters the sand a little behind the back entry line (right).

you're also laying the wedge face open to expose the bounce on the sole of the club to the sand.

As you can see in Figure 9-17B, my first practice swing entered the sand just a little too far behind the desired entry line. Not too bad (because sand shots have about a one-inch margin for error—a lot bigger margin than the Tight Lie shot #3—so relax!), but not perfect. Hitting one inch behind my imaginary ball would probably have resulted in a shot flying a little too short.

On my second practice swing, trying to hit another imaginary ball, my club enters the sand too far forward of the desired entry line (Figure 9-17C), which would result in a thin shot flying too far.

Figures 9-17C and 9-17D: My second practice swing hit too close to the ball line (left); my third practice swing produced a perfect divot (right).

My third practice swing (Figure 9-17D) is perfect. As you can see, my clubhead touched down exactly on my desired entry-point line, and my divot is about ¾-inch deep. The swing probably would've resulted in a pretty good shot. Now that I'm in a groove, it's time to hit the first real ball.

When you get to a real ball, you still want to imagine yourself hitting an imaginary ball sitting behind it (on the entry-point line), as if it were sitting on grass. This thought will help you to produce your normal wedge swing.

Good sand shots come from good sand swings, which create good sand divots. The Line Drill challenges you to hit ten sand

shots without missing the proper entry-point line by more than one inch with any of your swings. In our schools we have some students do this drill without ever hitting real balls, because there is no point in watching bad sand shots (which is all you will get) until you can make good sand divots.

TAKE IT TO YOUR BACKYARD

Backyard practice is a wonderful thing for any golfer who wants to improve. Once you figure out what to practice, and how to practice it, then doing it becomes the fun part.

The Pelz Golf Institute has developed two feedback devices to help with your backyard practice. The BunkerBoard and the PositionMat® provide two different surfaces from which to practice your sand game in your backyard. If you have either of these devices and some almostGOLF balls, you can learn the feel and rhythm of a good bunker swing at home.

Golfers who struggle with hitting sand shots fat (i.e., your clubhead hits too far behind the ball or digs too deep) need to practice with the BunkerBoard (Figure 9-18). It provides a hard plastic surface that will not allow your wedge to dig. By placing a small pile of sand on the forward end (opposite your left instep) of the BunkerBoard, one can experience the feel of one's clubhead sliding under and past the ball, and learn how little sand needs to be taken in a sand divot to produce a good greenside bunker shot.

Figure 9-18: AlmostGOLF balls fly realistically off the Bunkerboard.

For golfers who struggle to get their ball position correct in the sand, the PositionMat provides shoe outlines and the proper ball position in your stance. As with the BunkerBoard, you can hit almostGOLF balls from a small pile of sand off the PositionMat (Figure 9-19), and get the feel of a real sand shot.

Figure 9-19: An almostGOLF ball coming off the PositionMat.

For your backyard work to carry over into your real game, it's important that you understand that almostGOLF balls launch from sand on both the PositionMat and the BunkerBoard the same as real balls do from real sand. This can be seen when I hit three shots from the sand in Figure 9-20, the first two being almostGOLF balls off a Bunkerboard and PositionMat, and the third being a real ball from a sand bunker.

Figure 9-20ABC: AlmostGOLF balls react off the BunkerBoard (A) and PositionMat (B) similarly to real balls from real sand (C).

The point is, once you learn to play from the sand in your backyard, you can then also play the same shots with the same techniques on the course.

Backyard practice has been an effective tool for students who leave our schools—after having learned the fundamental setup and alignment rules for sand play. It allows them to practice their new-found bunker swings safely and conveniently. The benefits of back-yard practice are immense when it comes to the repetition and grooving aspects of conditioning your mind and body to see and feel good shots coming out of the sand.

I have found that very few amateurs take the time to drive to the golf course and practice their sand games frequently enough to get this kind of benefit. But I trust that you will take the time and effort to get the equipment you need to accomplish the task: either a BunkerBoard and/or a PositionMat, a bucket/bag of play sand, some almostGOLF balls, and a laundry basket for a target. After you assemble all of this in your backyard (Figure 9-21), all you need to add is the will to make it happen.

Figure 9-21: A backyard sand session blasting into a laundry basket.

Your assignment is to hit forty-eight almostGOLF balls per session, three days a week for two months. Each session will take you less than a half hour, and it can actually be lots of fun. To measure the progress you're making, set the laundry basket about 10 yards (ten steps) in front of your Bunkerboard or PositionMat, and count how many balls land in the basket in each session. (Balls that bounce into the basket from the ground or off the rim of the basket don't count. Balls that land in the basket but then bounce out do count.)

I know it's not the standard procedure to practice your sand game in your own backyard, but it's so much easier than going to the course three nights a week to do it. It's also time efficient, since it will only take you about thirty minutes each practice session (less than the driving time to get back and forth from the golf course).

If Eddie and I can practice in our yards (Figures 9-21 and 9-22), you can do it too. Try it. I think you might like it, and I'm sure your sand game will love it too!

OPPOSITE: Figure 9-22: Once you set up properly, practice will move you toward perfection.

CHAPTER 10

1

Most Feared Shot #1:
Short Putts

The Shot

THE THREE-FOOT PUTT (FIGURE 10-1) is often conceded during casual rounds of golf. It's considered a "gimme" because it looks so simple, but also because nobody wants to miss from so close. It's embarrassing to miss one and it costs a whole stroke!

Figure 10-1: The short putt.

By all measures, the short putting stroke is the easiest swing to execute in golf. The motion of a short putt stroke is small, you're close to the hole, and your margin for error appears to be pretty generous (Figure 10-2). The ball has a perfect lie, and you're always allowed to clean it before you putt. It won't break too much, and you won't hit it fat or thin. Research at the Pelz Golf Institute has shown that amateurs perform closer to the level of pros on short putts than they do on any other shot in golf.

So why, then, do three-foot putts inspire so much fear in golfers? Because golfers miss short putts every day—all around the world—with great regularity. Amateurs miss them, pros miss them, and we all anguish over our performance when we miss them. There is no worse feeling in golf than missing a three-footer, especially when a competition is on the line and that stroke *makes the difference*! It's hard to accept missing when you expect to make the shot (Figure 10-3). Perhaps this is why the short putt was voted by our survey golfers as the most feared shot in golf!

Any golfer who seriously cares about his or her performance and score will begin to worry about their short putts, especially once they notice that they're missing more than their fair share of them (Figure 10-4). There are more strokes attempted inside six feet than any other type of shot in golf: If you want to enjoy the game, you've got to be good at short putts.

The Problem

There are five main problem areas that contribute to the difficulties that golfers have with short putts. Each of these areas works in a different way to influence and increase the odds of missing a short putt.

Figure 10-2: Our Senior instructor Ty Waldron demonstrates how easy it is to pull a three-foot putt. Will it sneak inside the left edge, or miss?

Figure 10-3: With great anguish, Ty observes the wrath of the Golf Gods: the dreaded lip-out.

Figure 10-4: Missed short putts can make you *sick*! As misses increase, they become more expected. Anxiety grows into fear, and fear increases your likelihood of missing.

Few golfers suffer from all five problems. However, if you struggle with short putts, you must struggle with at least one of them, because there is *something* wrong with your short putting. The first order of business in tackling your problem is to identify and understand which weaknesses you have and which you don't. For this reason, you should become aware of all five problem areas listed below.

1. Poor green-reading (allowing for the wrong amount of break) causes you to incorrectly blame your misses on stroke mechanics.

2. Poor aim/alignment of your putter and stroke causes good strokes to miss and requires bad strokes to hole putts.

3. Excess forearm and putterface rotation through impact (especially under pressure) causes putts to start off-line.

4. Deceleration of the putter through impact makes putts more susceptible to the "lumpy donut" effect (e.g., footprints, scuff marks around the hole).

5. Mental anguish fostered by unreasonable expectations causes golfers to make poor-quality strokes.

GREEN-READING

When golfers miss short putts they don't usually blame their green-reading skills. But allowing for the wrong amount of break is often the cause for missing short putts, and it doesn't get its fair share of the blame.

Many golfers assume there is no break on short putts. Even though they know that slopes on the green cause putts to break, they resolve to take the break out of their short putts. I'm sure you've heard the phrase "Keep it inside the hole." While this can be good advice at times, it can also cause putts to be missed. Good green-reading is fundamental to holing short putts.

AIM AND ALIGNMENT

The stroke for a short putt is so small that there's little time for compensations to correct for bad putter aim or body alignment. When a golfer reads a three-foot putt to be straight in (and it really is straight), but then unknowingly aims his putterface to the left edge (Figure 10-5), he's not likely to make the putt. Putter aim and stroke alignment are fundamental to good short putting.

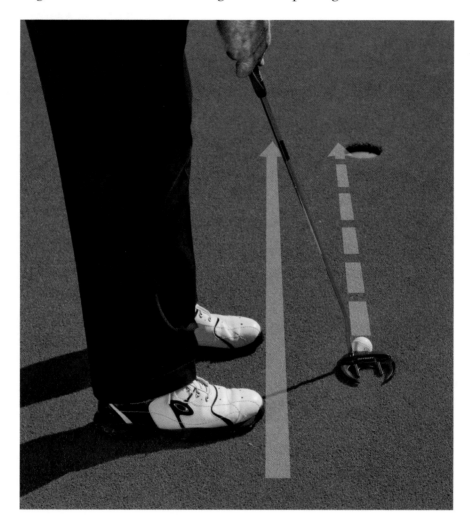

Figure 10-5: Poor body alignment and putterface aim can doom your short putts.

FOREARM AND PUTTERFACE ROTATION

Most golf swings require the forearms to rotate through impact to produce power, but not the putting stroke. The latter requires a good feel for distance, but not much force. Out of habit, however, many golfers rotate their forearms during their putting strokes. They don't think they do and they say they're not trying to, but their forearms do rotate (I'm sure of this, I've measured it) as they putt.

If a golfer normally rotates his putterface from open to closed during the stroke, it's highly likely that this rotation will happen faster when they get under pressure. This is the cause of many pulled short putts (Figure 10-6). A square putterface, which delivers a square strike to the ball, is fundamental to good short putting.

Figure 10-6: An early rotation of the putterface causes this three-footer to be pulled left.

DECELERATION THROUGH IMPACT

A putterhead that is slowing down will not contact the ball as solidly as one that is accelerating into and past impact. A decelerating putter transfers less energy to a putt than the golfer intended, producing a weak-rolling ball that often doesn't hold its line (Figure 10-7). You might think of it like this: "When a decelerating putter speaks, the ball doesn't listen."

Figure 10-7: A decelerating stroke causes the putt to lose steam and die off-line.

Golfers often make poor strokes—they pull and push putts, allow their strokes to decelerate, and aim poorly. And typically these things cause putts to miss the hole. Sometimes, however, golfers do everything right. They execute perfect strokes and still miss the hole. On these occasions, they don't deserve to miss their short putts, but that's the game we play. Putting greens are not perfect surfaces, and they sometimes don't allow balls to roll where they should. Footprints and spike marks exist, the wind blows, and sometimes the Golf Gods rule. Suffice to say: Well-struck putts sometimes miss, while poorly struck putts sometimes go in.

Golfers shouldn't worry about such things, but they do. They often have unrealistic expectations about their putting success, and this can cause real problems.

The Solution

To combat these problems and make a greater percentage of your short putts, you should embark on the following five-step short-putt improvement program.

STEP #1: IMPROVE YOUR GREEN-READING

You do have some margin for error with your green-reading. There is room in a 4¼-inch hole for three golf balls putted side by side to fall into the hole (Figure 10-8), assuming they roll at the proper speed. If you read the break of a three-foot putt correctly to within an inch or two, you'll make the putt, all other things being perfect.

But therein lies the rub. All other things are often not perfect. Therefore, if you can read the correct amount of break within a half inch, you'll be a lot better off. And while this may sound like it shouldn't be much of a problem, we find in our short game schools that it really is. Golfers have a lot of trouble reading greens accurately. They don't see green slopes well, and even when they know the slopes are there, they don't estimate how far perfectly rolled putts will break (curve) on their way to the hole.

There's no doubt: The better you read greens, the more short putts you'll make. In the next section I'll show you several ways to improve your skills

Figure 10-8: There is a decent margin for error when reading the break of a short putt.

in this area. And in the conditioning section at the end of this chapter, I'll give you drills to internalize these skills.

STEP #2: IMPROVE YOUR AIM

It doesn't do you much good to read greens well if you can't aim where you want to. Most golfers learn to subconsciously aim their putters to compensate for imperfections in their putting strokes. But then poor aim makes it difficult for them to improve their strokes, because when they do, they miss everything due to their aim. There is a solution, however. If you learn to aim independently from your putting-stroke mechanics, your stroke will automatically begin to improve over time. You must continue to aim accurately over this period of time (which takes practice), but the system does work.

STEP #3: MAINTAIN A SQUARE PUTTERFACE THROUGH IMPACT

The more you rotate your putterface through the hitting zone, the more difficulty you'll have getting it to be square at impact. It's like trying to arrive somewhere exactly on time: you're either a little late or a little early, but almost *never* exactly on time.

It's fairly simple, however, to develop a pure in-line square stroke (PILS)—sometimes referred to as a straight-back, straight-through stroke—that maintains a square putterface through impact (Figure 10-9). Most golfers rotate their putterface through impact because their forearms rotate subconsciously as they swing their arms past their body. They don't mean to do it, nor are they aware of it, but it's ingrained in them from their full-swing habits.

In the next section I'll show you how to groove the natural and much more effective PILS stroke.

Figure 10-9: A pure in-line square stroke (PILS) is much more effective from short range.

STEP #4: ACCELERATE THROUGH IMPACT

An accelerating putter directs the ball where to go. When a putter accelerates into impact, it maximizes its time of contact with the ball and helps to minimize the effects of off-center hits. You don't want quick or jerky acceleration in a putting stroke, just smooth acceleration through impact.

One way to learn to accelerate your putter smoothly is by putting in a "one-two" rhythm and making your follow-through longer than your backswing. Drills to help you develop the timing and length of such a stroke will be detailed in a later section.

Have you ever stopped to wonder why the Golf Gods deem that the game be played on greens with footprints and spike marks, where wind can occasionally deflect good putts off-line and bad putts back on-line? It's simple—they want to test your mettle, to see if you have resilience and can handle bad breaks. It will help your short putting if you accept the fact that you'll occasionally miss short putts, even when you stroke them perfectly. One can minimize the wrath of the Golf Gods, but never eliminate it entirely.

The best way to handle this is to expect to make every short putt, and to be surprised—but not shaken or ashamed—when you miss one. It will also help if you realize that putting greens are not perfect surfaces and sometimes don't allow balls to roll true.

The solution to your short-putting problem lies somewhere between two extremes. If you improve your skills just a little bit in the areas of green-reading, alignment, and stroke acceleration, and your capacity to deal with putts you miss, you'll hole a few more short putts. If you go further and drastically improve or actually perfect all of these skills, you might putt better than any human has ever putted before. The remaining sections in this chapter contain the information you'll need to determine where your short-putting improvement will fall within this spectrum.

How It Should Look

Through thirty-plus years of teaching, I've learned that once you have a clear intellectual grasp of *what* you're trying to learn, it becomes much easier to learn it. In this section, I want to show you the skills you need to learn, and how to learn them. The drills for conditioning your mind and body to conquer your fear of short putts, which constitute the actual *learning* you need to do, will be in the last section.

GREEN-READING IMPROVEMENT

To improve your ability to read putts, I want you to first understand how perfectly struck putts roll on a perfect green. In the test center behind my office I have installed several SYNLawn synthetic putting greens. A section of one of these greens is contoured with a smooth, 4-percent-grade slope. With a device called the True Roller (which can roll putts at perfect speeds in controlled directions), I rolled twelve three-foot putts from all twelve hourly clock positions around the hole and recorded the roll of each putt.

In Figure 10-10 you can see that only those putts from directly above and directly below the hole (the twelve and six o'clock positions, respectively) rolled perfectly straight. Every other putt had some break to it. I want you to also notice that the putts from four, five, seven, and eight o'clock (from below the hole) did not break as much as those putts from above the hole. In other words, downhill putts break more than uphill putts on the same slope.

Figure 10-10: Downhill putts break more than uphill putts on the same slope.

Another point to remember is this: If you pay attention to the amount of break your through-putt exhibits as it rolls past the hole (Figure 10-11, left), you can learn how much it will break coming back. It won't break the *same* amount, however, because you'll be rolling it faster coming back (you don't want to die it back to the hole).

Your comeback putt (Figure 10-11, right) will break about half as much as your through-putt, from about three feet. Your comeback putts will break a higher percentage of the through-putt break as they get longer than three feet.

Figure 10-11: At three feet your comeback putt (green) will break about half as much as the first putt broke after it passed the hole.

Watch how your first putt (or chip) breaks as it rolls past the hole. It's rolling over the same slope that your next putt must cover from the opposite direction. Given the right speed, your comeback putt will usually break about half as much as the through-putt.

One more thing: On short putts, speed is a critical factor. Putts tend to be rolling very slowly as they approach and pass the hole. The slower they roll, the more they will break (Figure 10-12).

Figure 10-12: The slower a putt rolls, the more it breaks.

AIM/ALIGNMENT

The worse you aim, the larger the in-stroke correction you must make to get the ball traveling in the proper direction. As a result, the better you aim, the better you'll putt. This is true for golfers of all handicaps (we've measured this performance correlation, and it is fact). Learning to aim accurately on short putts may well be the most important thing you can do to improve your short putting.

To help students who struggle with aim in our schools, we first use the Teacher Pointer (Figure 10-13) on their putterface. At one foot from the hole you cannot misalign the putter. As you move away from the hole, the red straw points the way and helps golfers learn to improve their putter alignment.

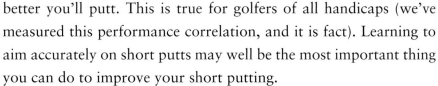

Figure 10-13: The Teacher Pointer helps you see where your putterface is aimed.

Figure 10-14: The LazrAimer shows a golfer when he's aiming to the left.

Another indoor training aid that helps golfers line up to their target line is the LazrAimer (Figure 10-14). You aim your putterface at the LazrAimer and it shoots (on voice command) a laser beam back at you that bounces off a mirror on the putterface and returns to the wall. The laser beam returns exactly above the LazrAimer (due to the putter's loft) to indicate perfect alignment.

By practicing your aim independently from your putting stroke, you can learn to aim properly in a matter of weeks (after aiming poorly for dozens of years). You must practice your putting stroke diligently during this time, however, to successfully reduce your previous in-stroke compensations and accommodate your new aiming skills.

FOREARM/PUTTER ROTATION

To consistently roll short putts well you must deliver a square strike to the ball. This means the face of your putter should be perpendicular to its stroke-path direction at the moment of impact. The short putting stroke should be as simple as you can make it. There should be no extra movements or time wasted standing over the ball before you putt. (Your pre-putt routine and ritual will be detailed in the conditioning section later in this chapter.)

To deliver your putterface squarely to the line of your putt, you must have it aimed there before you start your stroke. On the backstroke, you must not rotate the face open or closed from its square-to-the-line orientation. There is no time during this short stroke motion to rotate the face open or closed and then get it back to square at exactly the right time.

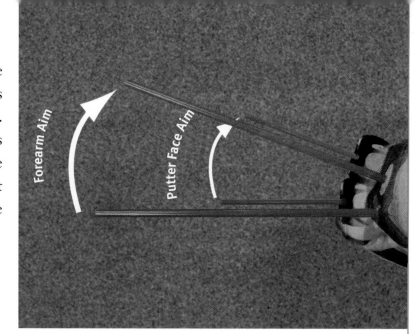

Figure 10-15: For right-handers, the back of your left forearm points in the same direction as your putterface at impact.

Some golfers have never thought of their forearm-putterface connection. The fact is, for right-handers, the back of your left forearm always faces in the same direction as the face of your putter. One is tied to the other (Figure 10-15). When you push a putt to the right you do so by aiming your left forearm to the right at impact; when you pull a putt to the left, you do so by aligning that forearm left at impact.

DECELERATION

Smooth, rhythmic acceleration is a trademark of a good putting stroke. By aiming your putter square to the putt line at address, and then taking a short backswing with your forearms and putterface square to that line, you set up the perfect scenario for holing short putts. If that backstroke is taken to the count of "one," and then you make a slightly longer through-stroke to the count of "two,"

Figure 10-16: The putterhead accelerates past impact in the perfect short putting stroke.

you will achieve a gentle acceleration to your putterhead through the impact zone (Figure 10-16).

If you can manage to keep your forearms and putterface square to your putt line throughout your through-stroke, you will achieve the perfect square strike on your putt. That is the best you can do. You can't make every putt, and you can't read the break of every putt perfectly, so you'll occasionally miss even if you stroke every one perfectly. Everybody misses, so don't worry about it.

REALISTIC EXPECTATIONS AND THE LUMPY DONUT

Part of the mental side of dealing with short putts is dealing with disappointment. Every golfer is disappointed after missing a short putt, but you can't let disappointment turn into discouragement or depression. You *know* that all golfers miss short putts from time to time. Even the best pros in the world miss short ones on occasion.

A serious cause of short-putt problems is a condition I measured and named over thirty years ago. This condition surrounds every golf hole where the green surface experiences a high volume of foot traffic during a day of putting. The condition is called the "lumpy donut." It exists on natural-grass putting greens around the world.

The lumpy donut is caused by golfers making footprints as they read, rehearse, and execute their short putts around the hole, and then retrieve their balls. When you consider how many good approach shots and first putts end up within a few feet of the hole, you can imagine how many footprints this can be. In the center of this area lies the center of the doughnut, a place no golfer sets foot in (either while putting or picking up balls from the hole). All short putts start from and must travel through the footprints of the lumpy donut.

Figure 10-17AB: A practice putting green hole in the morning (top), and in the evening (bottom) after many golfers have practiced their putting.

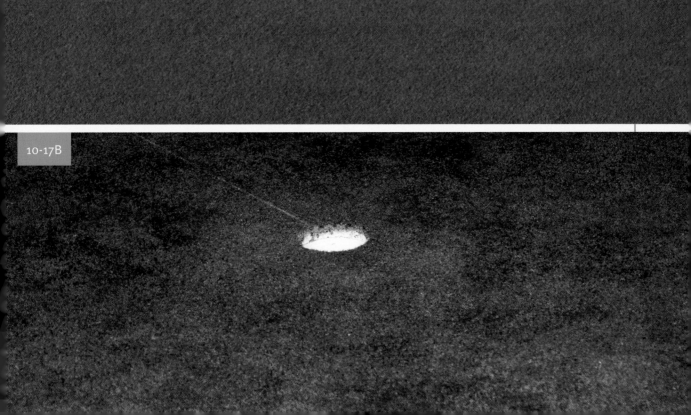

10-17A

10-17B

Believe me, I've measured them. Footprints exist and populate the lumpy donut. And to a golf ball, a ⅛ inch indentation is the same height as a five-inch roadside curb is to you. Have you ever tripped over a curb? Can you imagine a supersized, five-foot-ten-inch golf ball rolling through a parking lot of five-inch rocks and roadside curbs? Do you think it would roll straight? The truth is, short putts can be and are significantly affected and deflected by footprints in the green. The softer the greens, the worse the footprints. It's all part of the game, and there's no point in worrying about it. Understand it, but don't worry about it.

If you don't think humans leave footprint indentations in putting greens, then consider this: A green is a living, growing, manicured surface that is built to allow incoming shots to penetrate into that surface (seen any pitch marks lately?). Greens are watered frequently. Do you think a 300-pound boulder would sink 1/8-inch into the surface of the green? How about a 300-pound man with size 12 shoes, or a 140-pound woman with size 5 ladies' shoes (which may have way less green surface to support them)?

There is something simple you can do to minimize the effects of the lumpy donut on your short putts, and that is to position your ball about one to two inches forward of the bottom of your swing arc at address (Figure 10-18). This will impart a slightly upward strike on your ball. Don't hit way "up" on the ball, just launch it "slightly up" and out of the footprints. This will get it rolling on top of the grass, rather than through it.

Figure 10-18: Catch the ball slightly on the upswing to create the best roll on lumpy greens.

Additional Options

You can use any one of many putting methods (Figure 10-19) and become a great short putt putter with it. As long as you can read greens reasonably well, aim your putter where you want to, deliver a square strike to the ball, accelerate through the impact zone, and tolerate the occasional miss without going berserk, you can putt the short ones with the best of them.

10-19A

10-19B

10-19C

10-19D

10-19E

Figure 10-19:
Many strokes and grips can deliver a square strike and hole short putts:
A = Long Putter
B = Belly Putter
C = Left-Hand-Low
(for right-handers)
D = Saw Grip
E = Conventional

Success Examples

Short putting strokes are simple, but they are so important. They account for more strokes than any other shot in golf. That's why even the pros, who already have excellent strokes, practice them regularly. On days before and even during tournaments, you'll find them practicing short putts for hours on end (Figures 10-20 and 10-21).

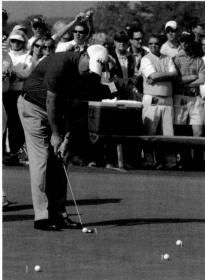

Figure 10-20: Phil Mickelson practices three- and six-footers at the Masters, the U.S. Open, the PGA, the Open Championship, and the Players.

Figure 10-21: Young PGA stars Nick Watney (left) and Hunter Mahan (right) practice their four-footers.

Conditioning Program

If you have a good intellectual understanding of the five-step putting stroke you're about to develop, and your mind's eye has a clear vision of what you should look like doing it, then all that remains to conquering your fear of short putts is to practice your drills. Each drill is designed to ingrain some skill, move, or feel into your body to form a habit of making good strokes, and to hole a high percentage of short putts. (Note: more information and detailed instructions on the use of all learning aids pictured in this section are available from www.pelzgolf.com.)

This sounds simple, and it is. But it will take time and practice, plus a good dose of patience, to accomplish the total task. You'll have to gather together several pieces of equipment to use in your living room or study and on your backyard or golf course putting green. In this practice, you'll need to execute a significant number of sessions before your new putting stroke can be trusted to replace the one that created your fear of missing short putts in the first place.

The goals of this program are to:

1. Learn to read the break in your short putts better.
2. Improve your aim (putter, body, and stroke).
3. Minimize forearm/putterface rotation and deliver a square strike at impact.
4. Accelerate through your short putts.
5. Ingrain reasonable expectations; do your drills.

GREEN-READING DRILLS

Step #1: Green-reading can be learned, but it takes time and energy: time to set up the equipment and learning aids, and the patience to watch attentively and learn as balls roll across the grass. Over the years I've developed two devices that teach you how to accurately read the amount of break in the roll of your putts.

They used to say green-reading was a God-given talent—you either have it or you don't. They said it could not be taught. But we've proven you can learn to read the break in your putts if you're willing to spend the time and effort.

The two learning aids shown in Figure 10-22 are the Putting Tutor and the TruRoller II. With the Putting Tutor, you aim a long white line in the starting direction for putts and then stroke balls along that line (guarded by two marbles to insure that your putt starts on-line). If the putts you roll through the marbles at good speed go in the hole, then you know the amount of break you played for was correct. If those putts miss, however, you know the break you played was wrong, so you have to re-aim the Putting Tutor and putt again.

Figure 10-22: Two green-reading aids: left = Putting Tutor, right = TruRoller II

The TruRoller II rolls putts on whatever starting line you choose, at an electronically selectable speed. By adjusting the starting line and rolling speed until you make putts at good speed, you learn the proper amount of break to play for putts. The more you aim and watch balls roll from the TruRoller II, the better you will learn to read greens.

Your assignment in Drill #1 is to set up one of these two green-reading devices and make putts with them. By spending one thirty-minute session per week for eight weeks, you'll have witnessed the proper amount of break on approximately five hundred putts. By this time the green-reading calibration in your mind's eye will have shown significant improvement in your green-reading accuracy on the golf course.

AIM DRILLS

Step #2: Your next assignment is to use one of our two alignment aids shown in Figures 10-23 and 10-24. In Drill #2 with the Teacher Pointer on your putterface, you'll putt ten balls inside a Putting Track toward a target in the distance (Figure 10-23). Block the roll of each putt with a book to keep balls from hitting and moving the target. Repeat this cycle six times for a total of sixty putts for each

Figure 10-23: Putt to a target with the Teacher Pointer on your putter.

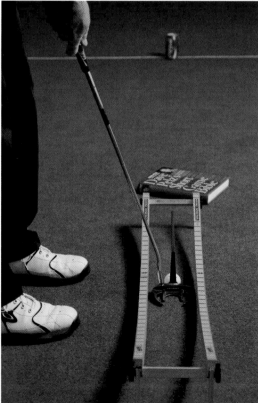

fifteen-minute session. Perform three sessions per week for four weeks, and move the target for each session to a different distance between three and twelve feet, in one-foot increments. All putts are to be hit with the Teacher Pointer on your putterface.

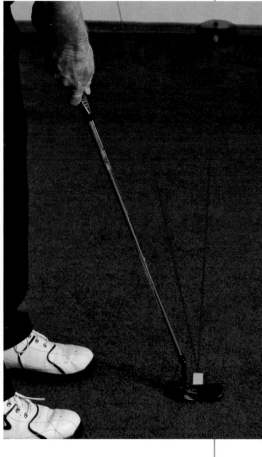

Figure 10-24: Learn to aim more accurately with the LazrAimer.

If you prefer improving your ability to aim using the LazrAimer (Figure 10-24), mark off distances with small pieces of tape at 3, 6, 9 and 12 feet from the LazrAimer. Then aim your putter from each distance, command the laser beam to turn "On" to check your aim accuracy (the beam will bounce off the mirror on your putterface), and move to the next distance. Complete this four-distance rotation ten times for one session. Test and check your aim three times (sessions) per week for four weeks.

SQUARE-STRIKE DRILLS

The O-Ball was created to help golfers develop square putting strokes, to start putts on-line with no sidespin. The O-Ball markings consist of four parallel rings—two around the ball's equator and two on its poles. The design concept is simple: Once aimed along its desired starting line, the ball will only roll without "ring wobble" if the putter strikes it squarely on-line (Figure 10-25). Any pull, push, or sidespin imparted to the O-Ball by a nonsquare putterface will cause the rings to visibly wobble as the ball rolls on the green and will tell the golfer about the deficiencies of his putting stroke.

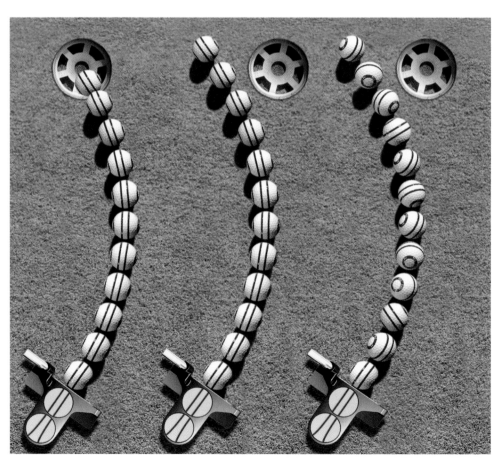

Figure 10-25: The O-Ball provides feedback after every stroke: left = squarestrike, good read; middle = squarestrike, bad read; right = bad stroke.

Every time you putt and see your O-Ball roll true, with no ring wobble, it means your putter delivered a square strike to the ball. As a result, you know your putt started rolling on the line you intended (the line you aimed it on). The more you putt with O-Balls, the quicker you'll learn the difference in feel between your good strokes and poor strokes, and the faster your putting stroke will improve (O-Balls conform to the USGA Rules of Golf).

Drill #3 consists of putting three O-Balls into a pillow three to six feet away, for a total of thirty putts. Each O-Ball must be aligned vertically (Figure 10-26) toward the pillow before putting. Once they are aligned, putt each ball in succession and watch as they roll. Each drill session should take approximately ten minutes. After four sessions per week for three weeks, your stroke should be delivering a high percentage of square strikes and pure rolls.

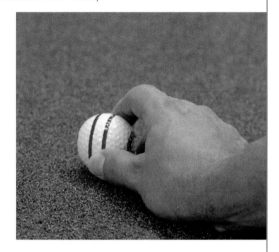

Figure 10-26: The O-Ball must be vertically aligned on the putt's starting line before putting, and is approved for tournament play under USGA rules.

ACCELERATION DRILLS

The easiest way to develop acceleration in your stroke while maintaining smoothness and good rhythm is to practice your stroke in an appropriately marked Putting Track. By this, I mean practice different-length strokes to the normal 1-2 rhythm of your practice stroke (one = backswing, two = follow-through), while making a slightly longer follow-through than backswing.

Drill #4 is to putt ten balls five times each in a session (fifty putts), three nights a week for two weeks. During this drill you must focus on taking the putter back a certain distance, as marked by a strip of plastic tape across the track (Figure 10-27). You must then swing the putterhead through to touch the appropriate tape on your follow-through, placed 10 percent farther from the ball than your backswing tape. With each session, change the length of your backswing by moving the tape, and adjust your follow-through to be 10 percent longer.

Figure 10-27: Putt in the Putting Track with backswing and through-swing marker tapes.

Always remember to use your natural stroke rhythm (repeat the 1-2 count to yourself) for practice swings, to set the rhythm of your real stroke.

THREE AND SIX-FOOT CIRCLE DRILLS (DEVELOPING REALISTIC EXPECTATIONS)

Drills #5 and 6—your final drills to conquer your fear of short putts—are the short-putt circle drills, which are designed to establish realistic expectations for success with three-footers on the golf course. By "realistic" I mean you should not expect to perform as well as the PGA TOUR pros—unless you practice as much as they do. Rather, you should expect to improve your performance on the course as you practice your drills.

Drill #5 is the three-foot-circle drill (Figure 10-28). In this drill, you roll three-foot putts to the hole until you find the straight downhill and uphill putts that don't break. There will always be two putts that don't break, which roll straight up- or downhill to the hole. Mark the straight uphill and downhill putts with two tees, then put four more tees around the three-foot circle on both sides of the straight putts (it's easy to measure a 3-foot circle by using a 7-iron with the clubhead stuck down in the hole). Now you're ready to place ten balls around the circle and putt them. Continue putting around the three-foot circle until you make ten in a row.

Figure 10-28: The three-foot-circle drill.

Drill #6 (Figure 10-29) is identical to Drill #5, except for two things: 1) All putts are from six feet, and 2) you don't have to make ten in a row. This drill is really difficult, so make as many of these putts as you can, but stop each session after about ten minutes.

Figure 10-29: The six-foot drill.

THE FINAL DRILL FOR THOSE WHO HAVE PUTTING "YIPS"

Golfers get the putting yips because they have stroke or aim problems, which cause them to miss too many short putts. If you have the yips, be sure to complete the drills described above, which will improve your green-reading, your aim, your forearm rotation, your ability to deliver square strikes to your putts, and your stroke acceleration. Then proceed to drill #7.

Drill #7 is our final drill, and it's reserved only for those golfers who have the putting "yips." It's really the same as the other circle drills, except that we use it from varying distances, starting at one foot. We start with eight one-foot putts around the hole (Figure 10-30). Begin by finding the straight uphill and downhill putts, but this time put three balls on either side of the fall-line (to form a one-foot radius circle). The objective is to putt for thirty minutes, starting with the one-foot-circle drill, and progressing outward as you complete each eight-putt sequence successfully (using a Teacher Pointer on your putterface).

You can't expand to the next longer putt circle (by one foot) until you make ten putts in a row at the previous length. Every time you make ten in a row you should move out to the next longer putt circle. If you do this drill for thirty minutes a day, three days a week for six months (and have continued to practice drills 1 through 6 during this time), you're on your way to becoming a short-putt demon on the golf course!

Figure 10-30: Start with a one-foot circle and extend outward.

A Tribute to
LEONARD KAMSLER:
The Man Behind Our Golfer's-Eye View™

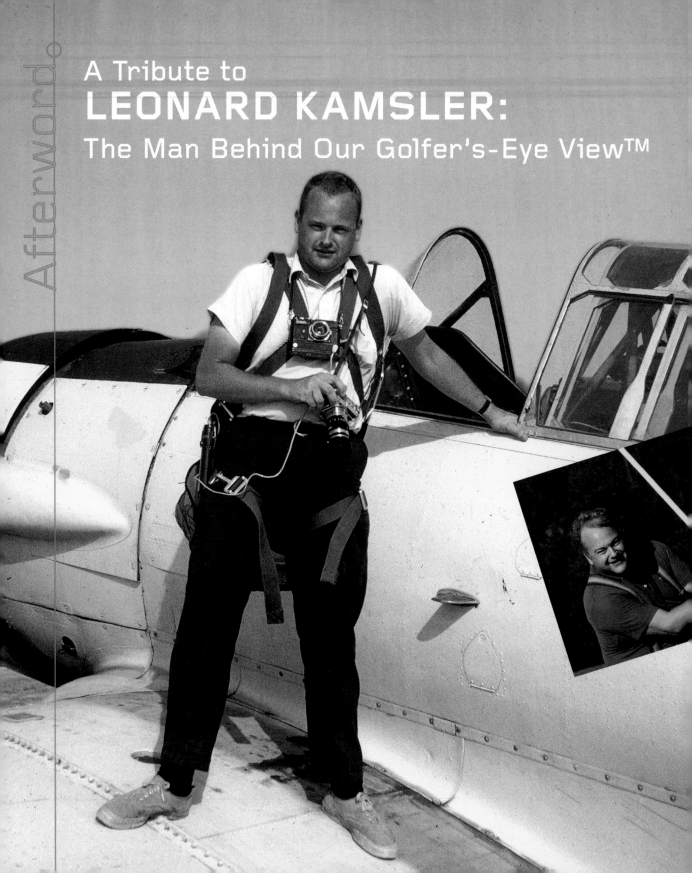

ON AN EARLY PHOTO SHOOT FOR MY PREVIOUS BOOK, *Dave Pelz's Damage Control*, I casually said to my photographer Leonard Kamsler (as Eddie held a mirror in front of my eyes and Leonard shot photos into the mirror from his knees, to show the position of my feet), "It sure would be nice if we could show pictures with a view as seen through the golfer's eyes. Can you figure out a way to do that?"

This was a long-overdue question, because since my very first golf shoot with Leonard more than twenty years ago, I've wanted to show golfers how things should look *to* them, rather than through the eyes of others looking *at* them. I'm sure instructors have always wanted this.

But every time a photographer stood in front of me and held a camera under my face, or tried to shoot from over my shoulders or behind my head, something always got in the way and screwed up the image. Because of this, most golf images in books and magazines have always shown face-on or down-the-line pictures that are looking *at* golfers. But sometimes these shots just aren't what the *golfer* (reader) needs to see.

For *Golf Without Fear*, I felt it was necessary that we show shots as seen through the golfer's eyes. This enables you, the reader, to actually "see" how your ball, feet, and stance should look, then instantaneously look up and see how the trees, water, or sand come into play in your shot direction—just like you do on the golf course. And by the time we started shooting for this book, my man Leonard had figured out how to do it. He had developed the "Golfer's-Eye View™" technology for creating the pictures we needed.

A BRIEF HISTORY

Figure A-1: Leonard as he prepared to shoot photos from the "tightrope walker's viewpoint."

It was Leonard Kamsler who originally adapted and used high-speed Hulcher cameras to create full-speed swing sequences of golf pros. He is also the photographer who first used strobe lights to stop golf balls on clubfaces and freeze the actions of golfers' swings. Widely regarded as the dean of golf-instruction photographers, Leonard has shot thousands of instruction articles and hundreds of covers for *GOLF Magazine*, including many with yours truly, over the last forty years.

Leonard is one who "exhausts all possibilities" (Figure A-1), as he did when I first asked him about the view as seen through the golfer's eyes. He said if we held a mirror at a 45-degree angle under my face and he shot directly "face-on" into the mirror, he would catch the clubface, my knees, the ball, and my feet. So we went to the hardware store, bought a mirror and photographed much of my *Damage Control* book this way.

Looking back at it, I guess this started the gears turning inside Leonard's head because he then tried small TV cameras, all different types of camera lenses and tripods and light stands to improve his technique, but none worked to his satisfaction.

THE DIGITAL CAMERA

Not long thereafter, Leonard found the key he needed to create views as seen by golfers. The first digital cameras arrived on the scene. He attached a small one to a long boom and his laptop computer, maneuvered the camera directly under a golfer's eyes, and shot the picture standing over his computer. Once Leonard informed me of his successful trial run, I flew him to California and we photographed several shots and named them our "Golfer's-Eye View™." The camera was not intrusive when positioned with my eyes looking through its lens, and its first image was of my lower arms and legs, feet, shaft, ball, and clubhead. From this he pieced together the rest of the shot (using markers to show where one image ended and the next began), all the way to the target. It was amazing! Leonard had done it again.

What's nice about the Golfer's-Eye View, besides being visually stunning, is that you can now see how your body relates to your target—plus all that stands between—as if you were there. It allows you, the reader, to "see" the shot without being on the course. This could never be done before in magazines and books, and it helps tell the story, which is what good instruction photos are all about.

LEONARD'S STORY

Leonard Kamsler grew up in Raleigh, North Carolina. After graduating from Duke University in 1957 he set out for New York City to become a professional photographer. He considered being a magician, but figured he couldn't make a living pulling rabbits out of a hat. But being a photographer wasn't easy, either. Leonard's first job paid $32 a week, $25 of which went toward rent. It was a job that many could only dream about, though, working as an assistant to Milton Greene (one of the most celebrated photographers in the world) at Marilyn Monroe Productions. The company had just finished production of *The Prince and the Showgirl* when Kamsler began his apprenticeship. Here he met the stars, from Marilyn, to Greene's "lunch buddy" Sammy Davis Jr., to Academy Award-winning British actor George Sanders.

Leonard was with Marilyn Monroe Productions for a little more than a year, then after a short stint in the Army, returned to New

York and started working freelance for *Sports Illustrated* and later with *GOLF Magazine* (located, by chance, nearby on 31st Street).

There weren't too many photographers shooting golf in the early 1960s, as evidenced by the fact that *GOLF*'s entire photo library could fit in one shoe box. Many of those photos were taken by Leonard, who began contributing on a more regular basis to *GOLF*, signing his first contract with the magazine in 1965. Golf was gaining in popularity and exposure at the time, thanks to the emergence of Jack Nicklaus and Arnold Palmer's legions of fans. As a result, *GOLF Magazine* began to focus more on players and instruction, and purchased a high-speed camera that could catch the best players' swings, frame by frame.

HIS QUEST FOR SPEED

Enter Leonard, with his technical expertise and penchant to "exhaust the possibilities" (at the time, GOLF's high-speed camera could shoot 25 frames per second). Leonard bought one of his own and began to tweak it to his preferences. He called Charles Hulcher (of the Hulcher Company) one day and said, "Is there any way we can make this thing go faster? How about 100 frames per second?" Hulcher replied, "You know, we might be able to do that."

One of the first sequences Kamsler did with his new 100 frames per sec camera was of Arnold Palmer. Over the years he shot many great players with the Hulcher, from Palmer, Nicklaus, Gary Player, Lee Trevino, and Tom Watson to Greg Norman, Nick Faldo, Annika Sorenstam, and Tiger Woods.

Kamsler also spent time with Harold "Doc" Edgerton (Figure A-2), learning stroboscopic high-speed photography at the Massachusetts Institute of Technology. Edgerton, a professor of engineering at MIT, was credited with bringing the stroboscope to photography. Leonard brought it to golf to capture a golf ball being compressed against the face of a club, as well as the spin of the ball as it then launched.

Typical Kamsler: Stroboscopic lights were not commercially available at the time, so Leonard returned home and built one. However, it only delivered 20 frames per second. So he created a device to take five strobes and alternate them to get the 100 frames per second he needed to shoot swing sequences.

The sequences you see in this book and instruction magazines are now shot with digital cameras delivering up to 60 frames per second. But for almost forty-five years, it was the work of Leonard Kamsler and Charles Hulcher, who made it possible to view the swings of the greatest players in the world.

A SPECIAL PHOTO

Kamsler photographed forty consecutive Masters tournaments from 1963 through 2002, and on the anniversary of his thirtieth, was presented with a caricature photo signed by all of the players in the field (Figure A-3).

Figure A-3: The players thank Leonard for thirty years of service at the Masters.

His most memorable photograph from Augusta was snapped in 2001, adjacent to the 18th green. The photograph is a panoramic photo of Tiger Woods's clinching putt (and fist pump), and also his approach shot into the green. It was Tiger's fourth consecutive major, making him the only player in modern golf history to capture consecutive U.S. Open, Open Championship, PGA Championship, and Masters titles.

"The scene at the 18th hole of the Masters is awesome when all those people come together on one hole," said Kamsler. "You can't get it all in one shot, but I put two images together and captured a very memorable event. I was lucky Tiger hit his drive to where I could see it, and he made the putt."

A SPECIAL MAN WITH MANY TALENTS

Figure A-4: The Kamsler Friendship Kup.

Leonard's work in golf photography is respected by players, teachers, and his peers. In 1991, the golf photographers' Ryder Cup (a biennial competition between American and European photographers preceding the actual event among professional golfers from the PGA and European Tours) was named the "Kamsler Friendship Kup" (Figure A-4). In 2001, he was awarded the Memorial Golf Journalism Award, presented to him prior to the PGA TOUR event that carries the same name.

While golf has been his primary focus, Leonard's talents extend beyond the game. He has photographed major country music stars from Johnny Cash, Dolly Parton (Figure A-5), Charlie Daniels, and Loretta Lynn to Waylon Jennings and Willie Nelson. His work was featured regularly in *Country Music Magazine* and on several album covers, including Cash's *Rockabilly Blues*.

Leonard has shot for Ringling Brothers' "Greatest Show on Earth," the Moscow Circus, Siegfried and Roy, Disney on Ice, Bolshoi on Ice, and the Harlem Globetrotters.

Figure A-5: Leonard and Dolly.

MY FRIEND LEONARD

My first photo shoot with Leonard occurred in October 1984. I had seen the strobe work he'd done and I needed to show a golf ball skidding the first several inches off a putter before it began to roll. I was told Leonard was the only photographer who could be trusted to get that shot. A friendship was born that day between two scientists, one in the short game and putting, and the other in photography.

Amazingly, the brains behind our Golfer's-Eye View concept—the man who practically invented golf-instruction photography—has never played a round of golf in his life. Frankly speaking, I've never even seen him hit, or even putt a ball! Not once. But believe me, he knows how to play the camera for this game better than anyone else. He is *the* virtuoso!

I count myself extremely lucky to be able to work regularly with the world's greatest golf photographer, and to be able to pay tribute to him here. I also feel privileged and honored to be able to count him as one of my close friends. And, finally, I'm grateful for the opportunity to share with you in this book the Golfer's-Eye View visions he produced. I think they'll help you become a better golfer!

Dave Pelz

Acknowledgments

I **WOULD LIKE TO ESPECIALLY ACKNOWLEDGE THE WORK AND SKILL** of Sven Nilson for creating the illustrations, adding art to our photographs, building swing sequences, as well as all the scanning, digital color corrections, and a myriad of other high-tech challenges involved with this book. I also send thanks to my friends Phil Mickelson, Paul Azinger, and Tom Sieckmann for their time and patience in letting us photograph their incredible golf swings and talents.

GRATEFUL ACKNOWLEDGMENT is made to Leonard Kamsler and Pelz Golf Institute for permission to reproduce their work. We also thank the members and staff of the Turning Stone Resort, Hamilton Farm, Hazeltine National, Escondido, and Bethpage Black golf clubs for their time and generous hospitality, in letting us capture the beauty of their golf holes in this book. And I especially want to thank my home club of Escondido (in Horseshoe Bay, Texas) for all their assistance in helping me to create several of the most feared shots.

DATE DUE

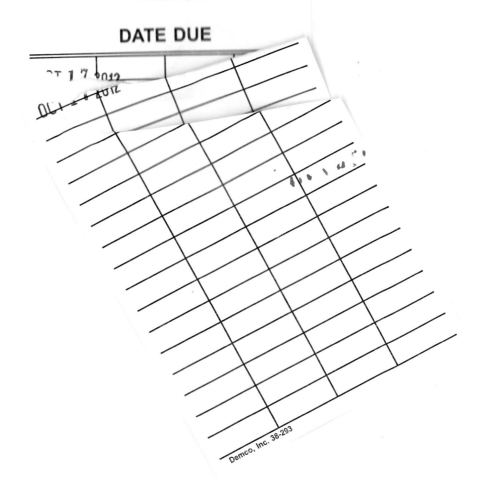

Demco, Inc. 38-293